I will never forget the day I was walking down the hall of my house and was literally pulled into my office by the anointing that was coming through the television. I stood there speechless watching a young woman with an old mantle ripping open the heavens and boldly approaching the throne of grace. I knew I was watching what has increasingly become a lost art in today's church. Pastor Kimberly Ray is the real deal, and this book is a *must-read* for everyone who desperately desires to experience the power of an answered prayer.

—SHERYL BRADY
PASTOR, THE POTTER'S HOUSE OF NORTH DALLAS
AUTHOR, *YOU HAVE IT IN YOU*

It's priceless when you know how to pray. *Spiritual Intervention* will be most valuable to everyone who wants to learn how to pray effectively! Kimberly Ray is anointed to intercede for you and for me.

—CECE WINANS
GRAMMY-WINNING RECORDING ARTIST

In an age and era too often characterized by the great sin of prayerlessness, God has used one of His finest vessels to bring genuine hope and healing to very real life situations. In her masterful book *Spiritual Intervention*, Pastor Kimberly Ray, God's woman of prayer and faith, provides abundant and therapeutic healing balm for the deep pain and wounds of our souls. Using keen Scripture-based insights and powerful experiences in the Spirit, this mighty woman of God will lead you to the rich oasis of deliverance and joy promised to all those who trust Him in prayer. It's a must-read for all!

—BISHOP HORACE E. SMITH, MD
PASTOR, APOSTOLIC FAITH CHURCH, CHICAGO, ILLINOIS

Spiritual Intervention is not just another book on prayer. It is written as a "breakthrough" manual that gives directions to those who must pray but know not what or how to pray. Every chapter is impregnated with the spirit of healing, deliverance, victory, and growth. *Spiritual Intervention* is the prescription for whatever is ailing those who seek to experience the manifested power of God, while yet being confronted by the vicissitudes of daily living. This is a road map for the believer's journey to an overcoming testimony that will bear witness to the greatness of our God throughout all generations. Without hesitation but with a deep sense of urgency I recommend this work!

—DR. CAROLYN SHOWELL
PROFESSOR OF OLD TESTAMENT AND RABBINIC STUDIES
THE BALTIMORE HEBREW UNIVERSITY

spiritual
intervention

Powerful insights for BREAKTHROUGH PRAYERS

KIMBERLY L. RAY

CHARISMA
HOUSE

Library of Congress Cataloging-in-Publication Data:
Ray, Kimberly L.
  Spiritual intervention / Kimberly L. Ray. -- First edition.
      pages cm
  Includes bibliographical references.
  ISBN 978-1-62136-550-1 (trade paper) -- ISBN 978-1-62136-
551-8 (ebook)
 1. Prayer--Christianity. 2. Intercessory prayer. I. Title.
  BV210.3.R38 2014
  248.3'2--dc23

                                        2013037844

While the author has made every effort to provide accurate
telephone numbers and Internet addresses at the time of
publication, neither the publisher nor the author assumes
any responsibility for errors or for changes that occur after
publication.

14 15 16 17 18 — 98765432
Printed in the United States of America

I dedicate this book to the memory of my beloved parents, Harry and Angie Ray. My mother taught me a pure love for fervent and passionate prayer. My father instilled in me a desire for a clean heart. Gratitude is what I will carry with me for a lifetime for three extraordinary treasures, my natural sisters Cheryl, J. Denise, and Tanya. Your incredible love, dedication, and remarkable strength have blessed my life beyond measure. Special thanks also to my executive assistant, LaWanda Rucker. Your perseverance is noteworthy. Lastly, to the Church on the Rock—you inspire me.

CONTENTS

Spiritual Intervention for Those Suffering From Addiction and Compulsive Behaviors

Spiritual Intervention for Families and Relationships

Spiritual Intervention for Health and Healing

Spiritual Intervention for Spiritual Breakthrough

FOREWORD

I AM EXCITED TO recommend this book on the power of prayer. I have known Kimberly Ray for many years. She has committed herself to prayer and deliverance, and her knowledge of the subjects has come from experience and seeing many set free. The teachings and prayers in this book will help many be delivered from the bondages and traps of the enemy. I believe that anyone who reads this book and prays these prayers in faith will experience the miracle of salvation and deliverance.

There have been many books written on the subject of prayer that have blessed the church. God is expanding our understanding of deliverance, and there are new prayer books being written that take us to another level of faith and breakthrough. This book has been birthed out of years of experience in dealing with difficult problems and strongholds. God has been gracious to us in giving us answers to difficult problems, and the results have been astounding. I challenge those reading this book to draw from the wisdom given by the Father through Kimberly Ray.

There are areas covered in this book that have not, to my knowledge, been covered in other prayer books. There are unique prayers for victims of violence and for military families. These two areas have become important because of what is taking place in the world today and the trauma that many have suffered as a result. There are also powerful prayers for children and men, both of whom have been targets of the enemy to weaken and destroy the family.

There has also been such an increase in the number of people with eating disorders, drug addiction, sexual bondage, and compulsive behaviors. Divorce and marital confusion are at record highs in our nation. Many people have suffered from abuse and need healing and deliverance on a deeper level. These problems require a spiritual solution. Deliverance is the solution that is urgently needed. The lack of deliverance teaching in many churches has left many without hope and solutions to these problems. This book will challenge you in the area of deliverance and prayer and give you hope when it seems hope is lost.

There are many who need deliverance from poverty and financial bondage. These are often difficult patterns to break for many individuals, and prayer and deliverance are necessary in many cases. Poverty will sap the strength from a person and decrease their desire to live. It is important to be set free from this stronghold, and strong prayers for deliverance need to be declared. This book has the prayers one needs in this area and will help those struggling to overcome these persistent strongholds.

Nothing is impossible with God. His wisdom is greater than any problem. God has given Kimberly keys that unlock the chains of bondage and set the captives free. You will be blessed by the prayers that cover areas that are often overlooked. There are also teachings that accompany the prayers that will give you a greater understanding of the power of prayer. I am excited to see a new generation of leaders releasing books that will be powerful weapons against the forces of darkness.

I pray this book will expand your prayer vocabulary and give you a greater authority to see breakthrough. These teachings and prayers will help you receive deliverance for yourself and give you the ability to pray for others. I pray the level of prayer and deliverance will continue to increase in our land and across the earth. This book will contribute to that increase and result in many miracles being released through faith and the power of God.

—Apostle John Eckhardt
Overseer, Crusaders Ministries, Chicago, Illinois

INTRODUCTION

Y OU'VE PROBABLY SEEN it on TV or in a movie: a man or woman walks into a room filled with family and friends. Someone steps forward, speaking in calm, gentle tones, to let the individual know they're worried—afraid even—that something terrible will happen if they don't do something about the drug use, the alcoholism, the compulsive disorder. The family is at the end of their rope. They're fed up with the broken promises and pointless excuses, and they're tired of watching their loved one systematically self-destruct. So they intervene; they step into the middle of the situation in hopes of setting their loved one on a different path.

I am no stranger to crisis situations. It has been my incredible honor to pastor a wonderful congregation in suburban Chicago and to pray with countless people as I minister at home and across the country. Our internationally televised broadcast, *A Time of Intercession*, also has been a vehicle to reach millions of people around the world with the gospel of Jesus Christ and to minister to those who call us in urgent need of prayer. A son is on drugs. A sister is caught in an abusive relationship. A friend has been diagnosed with a chronic or terminal illness.

The number of prayer requests seems to be growing as people contact us not only by phone and e-mail but also via Facebook, Twitter, and other social media. I meet others in the prayer lines when we host prayer revivals in cities across the United States. Many of the needs have been of such an urgent nature, my heart breaks as I cry out to God on their behalf.

It is because of the pain I have seen that I have written

this book. We serve an all-powerful God who has not left us without hope. We can pray for others even when they do not know how to pray for themselves. We can stage an intervention—a spiritual intervention—and bombard heaven until there is a breakthrough.

The Bible tells us, "Likewise the Spirit also helpeth our infirmities: for we know not what we should pray for as we ought: but the Spirit itself maketh intercession for us with groanings which cannot be uttered" (Rom. 8:26). As Christians, we are not rendered helpless. We have tremendous authority in prayer. We can stand in the gap and pray for yokes to be destroyed, blinders to be removed, and captives to be set free. We can intercede for the worst-case scenarios and watch the power of God change dismal circumstances.

What you hold in your hands is not just another prayer book. It is a manual for seeing breakthrough in prayer. The topics reflect the prayer requests most commonly received in our ministry. Each chapter provides insight into these common areas of bondage and offers specific prayer strategies to address the very core of the problem. I also explain how doors can be opened to the enemy, giving him legal access to our lives, and how we can close those entryways in the name of Jesus.

As you pray through the prayers at the end of each chapter, know that I am standing in agreement with you. Whether you are praying for yourself or someone else, it is a good idea to find others who will join with you in prayer. The Bible tells us, "If two of you shall agree on earth as touching any thing that they shall ask, it shall be done for them of my Father which is in heaven. For where two or three are gathered together in my name, there am I in the midst of them"

(Matt. 18:19–20). The power of agreement is a vital tool in your prayer arsenal.

Our God can do the impossible. He caused the sun to stand still so the Israelites could defeat their enemy. He parted the Red Sea to bring His people out of slavery. He opened up the womb of a ninety-year-old woman to fulfill His promise to Abraham. God has proved again and again that there is nothing too hard for Him.

We do not have to sit by, helplessly watching the enemy dominate circumstances and people around us. Jesus has given unto us "power to tread on serpents and scorpions, and over all the power of the enemy" (Luke 10:19). Proverbs 17:17 says a brother was born for the day of adversity. Together, children of God, we have the keys to defeat the enemy. Scripture says, "The effectual fervent prayer of a righteous man availeth much" (James 5:16). Because of the tremendous power of prayer, we can stage a spiritual intervention and see results.

Chapter 1
NOT BY MIGHT NOR BY POWER

I REFUSE TO BELIEVE that believers cannot obtain results through the power of prayer. Let us lay a foundation to the path of spiritual intervention by showing the power of the Holy Spirit. Spiritual intervention is allowing the power of God to flow through individuals who utilize intercession to obtain results for others who cannot pray for themselves. Despite the critical state of an individual who is standing in the need of intervention during a crisis, a spiritual intervention will address the areas that require the help of the Lord.

Before Jesus began His ministry on earth, God used John the Baptist to prepare the way for His coming. John's assignment was to preach repentance and "the baptism of repentance for the remission of sins" (Luke 3:3). During his time of ministry John the Baptist declared that he baptized with water unto repentance, but "he that cometh after me is mightier than I, whose shoes I am not worthy to bear: *he shall baptize you with the Holy Ghost, and with fire*" (Matt. 3:11, emphasis added).

Why am I so confident that God can intervene and change what may seem to be a hopeless situation? Because if you have accepted Christ as your Savior, you have someone you can call on for immediate help. His name is the Holy Spirit.

The Holy Spirit is many things to us. He is our comforter and advocate. An advocate supports and helps another. Immediate help to save, rescue, or provide assistance comes through the Holy Spirit. Many people try to fight their addictions, disorders, and bondages alone. If we had all of the answers, there would be no need for us to seek the Lord.

The Holy Spirit was given to help us. When we need help outside ourselves, we turn to Him.

The power of the Holy Spirit is explosive. In many places in Scripture the Holy Spirit is likened to fire. In fact, the Holy Spirit descended on the believers in the Upper Room as tongues of fire (Acts 2:3). If we are to be effective in prayer, we need the fire of the Holy Spirit. We need that fire to bring God's presence, His passion, and His purifying power in our lives.

God's presence. In the Book of Exodus, when the children of Israel left Egypt, "the LORD went before them by day in a pillar of a cloud, to lead them the way; and by night in a pillar of fire, to give them light; to go by day and night" (Exod. 13:21). In the same way, the Holy Spirit is always with us, protecting and guiding us, even showing us what things we ought to pray for (Rom. 8:26–27).

God's passion. Hebrews 12:29 tells us, "Our God is a consuming fire." The Holy Spirit desires to consume our lives, our thoughts, our will—everything. He wants us yielded completely to Him so that His words and His ways flow out of us and not our own fleshly wisdom and desires.

God's purifying power. In the Book of Isaiah the prophet had a vision of the Lord. When he saw Him, he recognized his uncleanness before a holy God and cried out, "Woe is me! for I am undone; because I am a man of unclean lips, and I dwell in the midst of a people of unclean lips: for mine eyes have seen the King, the LORD of hosts" (Isa. 6:5). Then an angelic being flew to Isaiah with a live coal in his hand that he had taken from the altar of God. The Bible tells us that after the seraphim laid the hot coal on Isaiah's mouth, he said, "Lo, this hath touched thy lips; and thine iniquity is taken away, and thy sin purged" (v. 7).

Fire has the ability to burn things up, and it is used to refine precious metals such as gold and silver. That is exactly what the Holy Spirit does in our lives. When we accept Him as Lord and Savior, He consumes the sin in our lives—which is anything that is displeasing to God—and cleanses our hearts so we can become pure vessels for Him to use.

The same fire of the Holy Spirit that fell in the Upper Room on the Day of Pentecost and guarded the Israelites as they left their place of slavery, the same fire that purified the prophet Isaiah's iniquity, is the same fire that dwells within the hearts of His people and produces boldness to war against the enemy. First John 5:14–15 says, "And this is the confidence that we have in him, that, if we ask any thing according to his will, he heareth us: and if we know that he hear us, whatsoever we ask, we know that we have the petitions that we desired of him."

We read in Acts 10:38, "God anointed Jesus of Nazareth with the Holy Ghost and with power: who went about doing good, and healing all that were oppressed of the devil; for God was with him." Jesus Christ was anointed with the Holy Ghost and with power. This is the power that enables us to command sickness and addiction to leave in the name of Jesus. It is the power that gives us strength to endure tests and trials and emerge victorious. It is the power that helps us resist the temptation to return to old vices and sinful habits, and to instead walk in the liberty Christ purchased for us on the cross.

The Bible tells us, "But ye shall receive power, after that the Holy Ghost is come upon you: and ye shall be witnesses unto me both in Jerusalem, and in all Judaea, and in Samaria, and unto the uttermost part of the earth" (Acts 1:8). In order to receive the gift of the Holy Spirit, one must accept the

Lord Jesus Christ as his personal Savior and believe that He is the Son of God who paid the price for our sins. If we confess with our mouths and believe in our hearts that Jesus Christ is Lord, we shall be saved (Rom. 10:9–10).

If we simply ask Jesus to come into our life and endow us with the power of the Holy Spirit, He will do so. This power helps us from day to day to overcome temptation and resist the negative influences of the past. This power rescues us in times of weakness. The Holy Spirit's power enables us to exercise restraint, walk in divine peace, and manifest the fruit of the Spirit (Gal. 5:22–23).

The power of the Holy Spirit is so great. The Holy Spirit is the one who enables us to walk uprightly. How does He do that?

The Holy Spirit empowers us to take dominion over every thought that would rob us of peace. Yes, that's right. We can ask God to regulate our thinking. Second Corinthians 10:5 states, "Casting down imaginations, and every high thing that exalteth itself against the knowledge of God, and bringing into captivity every thought to the obedience of Christ." This literally means that through the power of the Holy Spirit we can resist negative beliefs and replace them with edifying thoughts. For instance, if you wake up feeling depressed and heavy in your heart, you have the power to change the atmosphere by putting on "the garment of praise for the spirit of heaviness" (Isa. 61:3). You don't have to wallow in depression; the garment of praise will be like a cloak that surrounds you with the spirit of joy.

The Holy Spirit also empowers us to drive away the enemy. James 4:7 states, "Submit yourselves therefore to God. Resist the devil, and he will flee from you." The word *flee* means to run away from. The Holy Spirit gives us power to drive the adversary away immediately. After we have been set free of something, when the desire to return to that behavior tries to come back, we can do something about it: *resist*.

To resist means "to exert oneself so as to counteract or defeat; to withstand the force or effect of…by exerting oneself to counteract."[1] Don't give in to the temptation. Ask the Holy Spirit to help you, and He will do so the very moment you ask. Through the power of the Holy Spirit you have been given the strength to say no to the things of the flesh and the past.

Finally, the Holy Spirit gives us the power to live a consecrated life. To be consecrated simply means to be separated unto God for His glory. The Scripture tells us that we are to be different from the world. How do we do this? We are to "present [our] bodies a living sacrifice, holy, acceptable unto God, which is [our] reasonable service. And be not conformed to this world: but be…transformed by the renewing of [our] mind, that [we] may prove what is that good, and acceptable, and perfect, will of God" (Rom. 12:1–2).

After we have been forgiven and have received the gift of the Holy Spirit, on occasion the enemy will try to remind us of our past and the mistakes we've made. The Bible tells us, "If any man be in Christ, he is a new creature: old things are passed away; behold, all things are become new" (2 Cor. 5:17). So when the enemy tries to condemn us with our past mistakes, we must remind him of what God's Word says about us. Remember, "There is therefore now no condemnation to them which are in Christ Jesus, who walk not after the flesh, but after the Spirit" (Rom. 8:1).

The Holy Spirit has a remarkable way of working behind the scenes. I remember having my first real encounter with the Holy Spirit as a young girl, just twelve years of age. It was on a Friday night at a church in Chicago. Our pastor was teaching on the infilling of the Holy Spirit. His counsel to the congregation was that "the Holy Spirit comes into a glad heart." He instructed us not to ask for anything, but to simply praise God for who He is. That night, during our time of praise, I received an overwhelming, powerful infilling of the Holy Spirit. I remember feeling a spirit of peace, and I experienced for the first time speaking in a heavenly language. My mother was with me as tears streamed down my face.

I was still being blessed in the spirit when the person who brought us to church had to leave. My mother called a taxicab to give me time to continue receiving from the Lord. I was still praising God for the gift of the Holy Spirit. Even when I entered the taxi I was still receiving from the Lord. The cab driver asked my mother, "Is she OK?" She responded, "She is fine. She was filled with the gift of the Holy Spirit tonight." It is difficult to convey in words what I felt that night. I received an impartation of power and joy and an anointing. My life has never been the same.

It is the Holy Spirit who empowers us to live for God and to walk in His power. He is the one who gives us a tenacious desire to please God and not allow anything to break our fellowship with Him. And He is the one who helps us to daily resist temptation and the negative influences of the past. When we stumble, He will rescue us in times of weakness.

We never have to accept defeat when we have the power of the Holy Spirit. At a moment's notice we can call on the Holy Spirit and expect Him to come immediately to our aid. We claim the victory over the power of the enemy not by our might nor by our power, but by His Spirit, says the Lord (Zech. 4:6). Never—and I mean never—allow the enemy to convince you that your situation is hopeless.

Chapter 2
ARMED AND DANGEROUS

OUR ENEMY THE devil likes to see people in bondage; after all, his mission is to kill, steal, and destroy (John 10:10). People in desperate situations are right where the enemy wants them, and Satan won't let them go without a fight. That's why we must study or learn our opponent if we are to walk in freedom and see others set free.

Satan has positioned himself to show strong opposition against the body of believers. Unless we understand our adversary, Satan, and the wrath he has against us, we will not be able to defeat him. Webster's dictionary defines war as "a struggle or competition between opposing forces or for a particular end."[1] This opposition is not about you. The forces opposing you are really seeking vengeance against the almighty God.

When Lucifer was expelled from heaven, he convinced a third of the angels to rebel against the living God. As a result, all of them were cast out of heaven into outer darkness (Rev. 12:4), and a demonic hierarchy was formed—Satan's army. According to Ephesians 6:12, there are four separate entities in the kingdom of darkness:

+ Principalities
+ Powers
+ Rulers of the darkness of this world
+ Spiritual wickedness in high places

As we look at each area, you will see that the devil's kingdom is structured much like the US Armed Forces. In the military you have the commander in chief, followed by generals, colonels, majors, captains, lieutenants, and privates. In the kingdom of darkness Satan is the head and has ruling demonic spirits that are subject to him (see below).

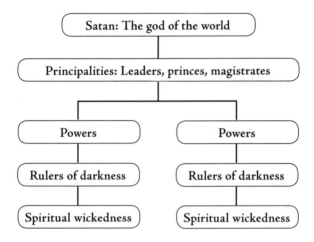

I want to take a close look at each of these levels of demonic authority.

Principalities

Webster's dictionary defines a principality as "the state, office, or authority of a prince."[2] As the above illustration shows, Satan is the commander in chief, and he has ruler spirits under him awaiting his command. Principalities are territories, regions, empires, kingdoms, locales, nations, countries, cities, or towns ruled by one with authority. Sinister supernatural beings are dispatched to govern such areas to carry out the destructive plans of Satan. We see an example of this in the Book of Daniel. In chapter 10 we read about a demonic principality that was specifically assigned to hinder the answer to Daniel's prayers.

> Then said he [the angel of the Lord] unto me, Fear not, Daniel: for from the first day that thou didst set thine heart to understand, and to chasten thyself before thy God, thy words were heard, and I am come for thy words. But the prince of the kingdom of Persia withstood me one and twenty days: but, lo, Michael, one of the chief princes, came to help me; and I remained there with the kings of Persia.
> —DANIEL 10:12–13

As this passage reveals, principalities may rise up against us, but we are not without help. Remember, God has given us His Holy Spirit, and greater is He who is in us than he who is in the world (1 John 4:4).

Powers

Power is defined as "possession of control, authority, or influence over others."[3] It implies the right to govern, rule, or determine, with the ability to wield forces. Demonic powers have been given authority over various regions to carry out whatever instructions have been given by Satan, the god of this world. Although Satan has power, God has given every born-again believer greater power. In Luke 10:19 Jesus said, "Behold, I give you power to tread on serpents and scorpions, and over all the power of the enemy: and nothing shall by any means hurt you."

Rulers of the darkness of this world

Rulers are princes of this age, magistrates who desire to control the world. Satan is the god of this world (2 Cor. 4:4). The intent of the rulers of the darkness is to govern the earth.

The Bible teaches us to "Love not the world, neither the things that are in the world....For all that is in the world, the lust of the flesh, and the lust of the eyes, and the pride of life, is not of the Father, but is of the world" (1 John 2:15–16).

This is why Jesus rebuked Satan when he offered Him the kingdoms of this world if He would worship him. As Jesus declared, "Thou shalt worship the Lord thy God, and him only shalt thou serve" (Matt. 4:9–10).

Spiritual wickedness in high places

These are demonic forces placed in strategic positions to rule over city halls, municipal courts, places of employment, schools, communities, villages, and the like. These demonic spirits have been positioned to infiltrate our world and its systems socially, politically, and economically. This is why it is imperative to pray for those who rule over you, as 1 Timothy 2:1–2 says: "I exhort therefore, that, first of all, supplications, prayers, intercessions, and giving of thanks, be made for all men; for kings, and for all that are in authority; that we may lead a quiet and peaceable life in all godliness and honesty."

THE WEAPONS OF OUR WARFARE

Despite the war Satan has waged against us, we have been given spiritual weaponry to protect, defend, and safeguard what rightfully belongs to us. No matter how organized Satan's regime may be, Jesus has not left us ignorant of his plans. We have been charged to put on the whole armor of God that we may position ourselves in opposition to the enemy. The Bible says:

> Wherefore take unto you the whole armour of God, that ye
> may be able to withstand in the evil day, and having done all,

to stand. Stand therefore, having your loins girt about with
truth, and having on the breastplate of righteousness; and
your feet shod with the preparation of the gospel of peace;
above all, taking the shield of faith, wherewith ye shall be
able to quench all the fiery darts of the wicked. And take
the helmet of salvation, and the sword of the Spirit, which
is the word of God.

—Ephesians 6:13–17

The apostle Paul wrote many of his epistles while a pris-
oner of Rome. During his captivity he was able to observe
the protective armor the Roman soldiers who guarded him
used. In the passage above, Paul used the armor to explain
how Christians can defend themselves against the vicious
attacks of our adversary. Let's take a look at each component
of the Roman soldier's armor and see how it relates to our
spiritual armor.

Loins gird about with truth

In a Roman soldier's armory the belt was essential in
keeping the other pieces of armor in place. From the belt hung
specialized hooks and holders to secure the casing that contained the sword and the quiver, as well as a device on which
to rest the large battle shield. Additionally, there were clips on
the belt that held the breastplate in its proper place.

In Ephesians 6:14 Paul is telling us that truth keeps the
rest of our spiritual armor in place. Operating in truth
allows us to be unhindered in warfare. It allows us to be
open to God in every area of our lives. In the natural we
gird up the loins by preparing ourselves for something that
requires readiness, strength, or endurance. In much the
same way, Satan will use any untruths in your life to expose
you and attempt to reduce your credibility as a Christian. If

you know the area of your vulnerability, close sin doors, and confess any hidden thing that is not like God, the enemy will not be able to silence you. However, if you are operating in truth, there is nothing for Satan to expose. We can boldly declare, "For the prince of this world cometh, and hath nothing in me" (John 14:30).

Breastplate of righteousness

The breastplate covered the chest and protected the Roman soldier's vital organs. Each breastplate was custom made. The believer's breastplate is not made of iron but of righteousness. Righteousness through Jesus Christ allows us to stand before demons with boldness and assurance that we have the victory. If you don't have certainty that you have been made righteous through Jesus's sacrifice on the cross, missiles of condemnation, accusations, and lies will penetrate your heart.

Feet shod with the preparation of the gospel of peace

The Roman soldier's sandals were not normal footwear. They were elaborately cut. The soles consisted of layers of metal and leather with hobnail spikes that would plant into the ground and give the soldier stability.

Even in our modern times, shoes ensure firm footing, mobility, and protection. Ultimate victory over Satan requires that we remain "stedfast, unmoveable, always abounding in the work of the Lord" (1 Cor. 15:58). Our shoes allow us to take an unmovable stance against our opponent.

Shield of faith

The Roman soldier's shield was comprised of six layers of thick animal hide. The layers were especially tanned and woven together, making them as tough and durable as metal yet lightweight. The shields could be soaked in water before battle so that if the enemy rained fiery arrows upon them, the fire would be extinguished on impact when it hit the shield.

Likewise the shield of faith protects us by repelling blows from the enemy. If the enemy can make us doubt God, he can get our shield of faith down far enough to get in one of his fiery darts and cause detriment to the soul.

Helmet of salvation

The Roman soldier's helmet was designed to deflect blows from the sword, hammer, or ax while allowing the soldier to maintain maximum visibility. The helmet of salvation protects your mind. If you are caught without your spiritual helmet, Satan can gain access to your mind, which will affect your actions and your emotions because our attitudes and behavior stem directly from our thoughts.

Sword of the Spirit

The Roman soldier's sword was a fierce weapon. It was short, lightweight, well balanced, sharp, and deadly. When the sword of the Spirit, which is the Word of God, is spoken in faith, it is a terrifying weapon to the kingdom of darkness. Hebrews 4:12 says, "The word of God is quick, and powerful, and sharper than any twoedged sword, piercing even to the dividing asunder of soul and spirit, and of the joints and marrow, and is a discerner of the thoughts and intents of the heart."

You may have noticed that all of the armor in our spiritual arsenal is defensive except this one. The sword of the Spirit is our only offensive weapon. That is why we must know the Word of God. It does more than protect us from the enemy's attacks; it changes the situation, puts the enemy to flight, and brings the victory.

THE POWER OF AGREEMENT

God has given us another weapon in our arsenal. It's called the power of agreement. In the Gospel of Matthew Jesus told His disciples, "Again I say unto you, that if two of you shall agree on earth as touching any thing that they shall ask, it shall be done for them of my Father which is in heaven. For where two or three are gathered together in my name, there am I in the midst of them" (Matt. 18:19–20).

God does amazing things when two or more people who believe God answers prayer speak the same request together in unity and in faith. Two or more individuals who are standing together in faith, praying in line with the plan and purpose of God, will see real results.

Here is a practical illustration of the power of agreement. In 1992, during the Olympic Games in Barcelona, Spain, an American named Derek Redmond was competing in the 400 meter race. He was the favored runner, so there was high expectation in the stadium that he would win the gold. Halfway through the race he ruptured his hamstring and could barely walk, much less run. In excruciating pain, he quickly fell behind as the other runners began passing him one by one.

After months and months of training, Derek was understandably devastated, but he had a relentless determination. Despite the enormous pain, he limped toward the finish line, excruciating step by excruciating step. Even now I remember how the atmosphere shifted when the crowds saw his father, who had been watching from the sidelines, run out and join him on the track. Placing his arm around his son, the father walked with him across the finish line.

That is the power of agreement. "Two are better than one;

because they have a good reward for their labour. For if they fall, the one will lift up his fellow: but woe to him that is alone when he falleth; for he hath not another to help him up....A threefold cord is not quickly broken" (Eccles. 4:9–10, 12).

Proverbs 17:17 says a brother was born for the day of adversity. Your prayer partners are there to support you when your faith gets weak or you grow weary in prayer. And if our prayers are like missiles raining down on the enemy, the writer of Ecclesiastes is telling us that by joining in unity, we are making those missiles even more powerful.

If we want to be strong in prayer, we must not only stand in agreement with others; we must also stand in agreement with the Word of God. The Word of God is the will of God. Agreeing with God's Word and declaring that truth in prayer will cause His power to manifest in our lives. Praying God's Word releases His will for the situation.

There is a direct contrast, the very antithesis of praying in faith. Just as we can choose to agree with God's Word, we can choose to agree with the enemy. Instead of standing on God's Word, we can believe the devil when he tells us our loved one will never be free of drug addiction or will never be healed or will never break away from that abusive relationship. If we stand in agreement with the devil, we reinforce his will for the situation and hinder our own prayers. That is why we must dig into God's Word to know His will, and then pray against anything that stands against His plans and purpose.

How do we do this? The Bible says we have authority to bind and loose (Matt. 16:19). To bind means to restrict, stop, hinder, arrest, or put a stop to. To loose means to untie, unbind, unlock, or liberate. We can bind the works of darkness, which include sickness, disease, hurt, witchcraft, poverty, death, destruction, confusion, defeat, and discouragement. And we can loose ourselves and others from the works of darkness. This will allow us to walk in greater liberty and prosperity. Jesus came to destroy the works of the devil and that we might have life and that more abundantly.

In the story of Derek Redmond we see another powerful illustration. Just as Derek's father was standing by ready to help, so it is with our loving heavenly Father. He is always standing close by, even when we don't feel Him near, and it is His good pleasure to reach out to help us.

Don't give up. Pray without ceasing. The Bible says man should always pray and not faint. Proverbs 24:10 says, "If thou faint in the day of adversity, thy strength is small." To faint is to lack vigor and strength. It is also to lack clarity or distinction. Remember that God is faithful. He has all power and the mercy to facilitate the change you are asking for. You are more than a conqueror through Him who loved us (Rom. 8:37).

You're in the Army Now!

In the United States we have what is called a volunteer army. Except during critical times of war when the nation institutes a draft, individuals choose whether to enlist in the armed forces. That is not the case with the Lord's army. As Christians, we each have a vital role to play in God's army. We must rise up and put on the whole armor of God, because our opponent daily lurks about devising ways to conquer each of us, our families, churches, cities, counties, and nation. (See 1 Peter 5:8.)

For that reason, there is no place in this spiritual battle for:

+ **Spectators**—those who watch from the sidelines with morbid fascination or who allow others to do their fighting
+ **Retired generals**—those who are often found mourning the loss of the good old days "when we would shut in and pray all night," rather than praying for the Lord to bring a passion for prayer back into His church
+ **AWOL (absent without leave) soldiers**—those who leave their spiritual posts and rarely go to church
+ **MIA (missing in action) troops**—those who are backslidden in heart

This spiritual battle can leave us with scars. But we cannot become resentful when injuries are dealt to us. We must get back up and continue the fight. No weapon formed against us shall prosper (Isa. 54:17). That doesn't mean the weapon won't be formed. It doesn't mean we won't feel the heat of battle. It doesn't mean we won't want to give up sometimes. It means the weapon won't succeed.

We are called to stand in the gap for those caught in Satan's clutches. We do not have to accept defeat. We do not have to think the situation will never change. Let's stay alert and on active duty to tear Satan's kingdom down!

Spiritual Intervention for Those Suffering From Addiction and Compulsive Behaviors

Chapter 3
ALCOHOLISM

M Y FATHER WAS a wonderful person. Dad had a special way with people and would light up a room the moment he entered. Daddy loved to laugh, and he loved his family. He worked hard to provide for my mother, my three sisters, and myself, but it wasn't easy.

He landed a fantastic job in Chicago as a butcher for a meat packing plant. He was a knowledgeable and skilled butcher and could answer any question about a cut of meat. Daddy was proud of his job, and he genuinely enjoyed his work.

Then suddenly the economy took a sharp downturn. The company was forced to downsize and laid off a great number of butchers, including my father. After Daddy lost his job, the disappointment began to take its toll. Daddy used to take an occasional drink, but after his company was downsized, he began to drink heavily. The Bible says, "Wine is a mocker, strong drink is raging: and whosoever is deceived thereby is not wise" (Prov. 20:1). We certainly saw the truth of that scripture in our family.

Daddy went from interview to interview, searching for a new job, but with each rejection he became increasingly disappointed, frustrated, and troubled, and he drank more and more as a result. Once a mild-mannered guy, Daddy became a different person when he was drinking. He could be combative and angry, sometimes taking his anger out on my mother.

I remember one night in particular. My dad came home from an evening of drinking, and my mother was sitting on the side of her bed. Without provocation he grabbed my mom by her long, black hair and wrapped it around his hand. Then he pulled his other fist back to strike her. Mom was truly a godly woman. That night she responded with a soft answer. Mom's wisdom turned away his wrath, and she was able to reason with my dad.

Prayer intervention is precisely what happened in our home. During volatile moments my mother prayed. She also taught her children to pray fervently each day for our father.

I remember once my baby sister, Tanya, who had been praying sincerely that Dad would stop drinking, found a bottle of his vodka hidden in the food pantry behind some canned goods. Though she was very young, in an act of faith she poured out the vodka and replaced it with water. You can imagine what Dad felt when he went to drink it and discovered it was water. "*Tanya!*" he yelled. It could have turned into a tragic moment, but my father reined in his anger and forgave her because she was the baby of the family and they were very close.

Every day my mother would put her hand under my father's pillow and quietly pray, "Father, in the name of Jesus, deliver, Lord!" At one point my mother received a prayer cloth that our pastor had anointed. Knowing the verse in Acts that says Paul the Apostle gave out handkerchiefs and illnesses were cured and demonic spirits left individuals (Acts 19:12), Mom sewed the prayer cloth to my father's pillow without his knowledge.

One night during one of my father's drunken stupors, Mom quietly watched as Dad opened the pillowcase and removed the prayer cloth, tossing it to the floor. In that moment it became crystal clear that a demonic spirit was influencing his behavior. Demonic spirits are aware of the anointing.

After our years of interceding for my father and believing God for his total deliverance, Daddy gave his life to Jesus

Christ. Dad never entered a twelve-step program or a reha-
bilitation facility. It was the power of prayer that changed
him. He later testified, "I don't know when it happened, but
God took the taste of alcohol from me, and the smell of it
makes me sick!" He acknowledged the sincere prayers of his
family as the reason for his deliverance from alcoholism. It
wasn't by his might or power but by the Spirit of God that
Dad was delivered.

What Is Deliverance?

Deliverance is bringing oneself into conformity to the image
of Jesus Christ by denouncing all satanic influences in your
life. It is a process of expelling demonic spirits to eliminate
all hindrances to your spiritual development.

Demonic spirits enter through "open doors." When we
commit sin, it gives the enemy a legal right to affect us in one
area or another. Unholy thoughts are one way doors open to
demonic spirits. After a person entertains the thought long
enough, the enemy plants a desire in the person to engage in
that activity, and engaging in that sin opens a door leading the
person into deeper bondage.

Whether through sins of omission or commission,
demonic spirits will enter when given the opportunity. A
good example is found in Matthew 16. When Jesus began
predicting His death, Peter responded by saying, "Be it far
from thee, Lord: this shall not be unto thee" (Matt. 16:22).
But Jesus knew the plan of God was to save humanity from
sin through His death on the cross. So He told Peter, "Get
thee behind me, Satan: thou art an offence unto me: for
thou savourest not the things that be of God, but those that
be of men" (v. 23).

That may seem harsh, but Jesus's response illustrates just

how subtle yet dangerous the enemy can be. In this passage of Scripture Peter had yielded to the temptation of the flesh. Just a few verses earlier Peter had received revelation from the Spirit of God that Jesus was the Christ (v. 16). After Peter declared Jesus to be the Christ, Jesus blessed him and said, "Upon this rock I will build my church; and the gates of hell shall not prevail against it" (v. 18). Yet by verse 22 Peter had allowed Satan to infiltrate his thoughts and spoke according to his flesh.

The devil is always around to tempt the saints of God. It is up to us, however, to submit ourselves unto God and resist the devil, knowing that he must flee (James 4:7).

The aim of deliverance is to remove the trespassing demonic spirits from the soul and body so that Jesus can reign over these areas. Deliverance is a way to eliminate the hindrances to our spiritual development. We read in 2 Timothy 2:21, "If a man therefore purge himself from these, he shall be a vessel unto honour, sanctified, and meet for the master's use, and prepared unto every good work." As saints of God, we do not have to fear deliverance. It is simply used to purge us from all filthiness of the flesh.

Deliverance is for all, but sinners cannot maintain their deliverance. An unbeliever must first receive salvation; otherwise the doors allowing access to the demonic spirits will remain open, and they will return. Christians, on the other hand, can be taught to maintain their deliverance by living a life sanctified and holy unto God. As 2 Corinthians 7:1 says, "Having therefore these promises, dearly beloved, let us cleanse ourselves from all filthiness of the flesh and spirit, perfecting holiness in the fear of God."

Deliverance is the children's bread (Matt. 15:26); therefore, we can pray in faith for God to deliver anyone suffering from alcoholism or any other addiction. We serve a mighty God who is willing and able to set the captives free. Let's pray together.

Prayer for Alcoholics

Gracious and loving God, we pray that You will extend Your compassionate hand of mercy to every individual struggling with alcohol addiction. Lord, we release Your power to destroy the root of this addiction. We pray that they will have the humility to acknowledge that they have a problem and need Your help. We ask that You give them strength and courage to fight for their lives and their families. Give them the will to reach for You in this crisis and to know that You have given them power to overcome.

Lord, we pray that You will reveal the moment the door opened to this addictive behavior. By the power of God we close every open door that has fed this bondage. Today in the name of Jesus Christ, according to the Word of God, we arrest the desire to run away from life's problems by drinking. We come against all shame, embarrassment, pride, and every spirit of fear. In the name of Jesus we bind all regret and refusal to forgive for past failures. We bind the strongman of alcoholism that temporarily numbs the pain. We break the dominating power of alcoholism and addiction over the mind, will, and emotions, and we trust You, Lord, for total freedom from alcohol addiction. In Jesus's name, amen.

Chapter 4
HOARDING AND COMPULSIVE BEHAVIOR

I N RECENT YEARS the word *hoarding* has become a familiar term. Cameras have been allowed behind closed doors to show how serious a problem this can become. In some homes piles and piles of trash are taking over people's lives. I would have thought this was a rare problem being exploited for TV ratings, but I am shocked by the number of prayer requests I receive from individuals who know someone suffering from this disorder.

Most people have a hard time understanding how a person can allow their "collection" of items to get so out of control that it takes over his or her living space. Not only do they not want to stop accumulating items, but they also don't want to let go of what they already have. From the outside looking in, it is mind-boggling to witness. The exterior of a home may seem average, but inside there are countless stacks of old newspapers, piles of clothing (some of which still have store tags on them), an overabundance of pets, unattended animal feces, and garbage in every room. Normal walking space has been replaced by narrow paths cut through rooms that epitomize complete chaos.

Naturally one would ask, "How can a person possibly live like this? How can he survive surrounded by loads of old books and letters, holiday ornaments, and 'collectible' items that are only valuable to the person collecting them?" There is always a root issue. Sometimes a traumatic event can bring on this kind of behavior. A major devastation can lead a person into depression, and they may find comfort in the stuff they accumulate. It can also stem from years of pain or repressed emotions that a person releases through hoarding.

A fascinating thing occurs when a hoarder is forced to deal with the clutter. It may be that the health department wants to condemn the home because of the potentially hazardous living conditions. Or perhaps some family members stepped in out of concern for a loved one's safety with fire hazards all around. Whatever the motivation behind the intervention, they are usually met with a strong spirit of opposition from the hoarder.

This is because there is a spirit of control at work. In the natural the hoarder is seeking to protect the massive accumulation of items, but in the spirit there is a demonic spirit seeking to maintain control of the individual in crisis. Those who come to help clear out the clutter are perceived as threats, so they are usually met with anger, hostility, and blatant resentment. The hoarder will try to personally observe, review, and revisit every individual piece others want to put in the trash. And he may say he feels violated by the perceived arrogance of anyone trying to discard or devalue his possessions.

What may seem like a simple task—throwing items into the garbage—becomes an all-out war. There is often a verbal battle, a true contest of wills between the hoarder and any person assigned to bring order to the home. The hoarder may even break down into tears and express hurt and frustration over the lack of sensitivity displayed by those assigned to clean his or her home. This is because the cleanup process is debilitating to the hoarder.

This kind of problem often divides families. Because there is no clean space available, the family is unable to sit together in one room to have a decent meal. Many times there is not even a clean place on the stove to cook. The environment often seems repulsive, and the hoarder is left alone in those conditions because he or she refuses to leave it. As one might imagine, this can leave the hoarder feeling lonely and isolated—ripe conditions for the enemy to wreak havoc on a person's mind.

Hoarding is just one type of compulsive disorder. I once met a woman who liked to eat chalk. Yes, the stuff we used as children to write on the school blackboard was the very thing this lady desired to eat all day. It is one thing to have an iron deficiency that causes cravings for unusual things such as ice, but this obsession for chalk could lead to intestinal obstruction and surgical emergencies.

It takes incredible patience, prayer, and compassion to help hoarders and those with other compulsive behaviors to find healing. This is because they often don't see the problem, which causes matters to only get worse. Fortunately God has an answer for hoarding and all compulsive disorders. Prayer can break the power of this bondage and free those who feel they cannot stop their self-destructive behavior. Jesus declared, "If the Son therefore shall make you free, ye shall be free indeed" (John 8:36). Let us pray in faith for the chains of controlling compulsive disorders to be broken in the name of Jesus.

PRAYER FOR THOSE SUFFERING FROM COMPULSIVE BEHAVIORS

Heavenly Father, we pray now for individuals who have experienced devastating trauma in their lives and have developed compulsive behaviors as a result. We speak to the place where the pain entered. We pray for each person

who has been unable to move forward. We ask You, Lord,
to touch their hearts and minds. Give them the courage to
allow others to help them in their time of crisis.

We bind the strongman of control and domination
and all mind-binding spirits that make a person unable
to think clearly and make simple decisions. We break the
spirit of anger and retaliation directed toward any person
sent to help. We come against the fear of loss, the spirit
of defeat, and fear of rejection in Jesus's name. We bind
the stronghold in the mind that magnifies loss. We speak
to the feeling that personal accumulated items are being
devalued. We break the mental and emotional ties that
prevent a person from throwing unneeded items away. We
bind false joy that manifests when a person repetitively
buys things he or she never uses. And we break the spirit
of poverty, wantonness, and mishandling of finances.

We bind every spirit of rejection and isolation, and the
feeling that makes someone think no one loves him. And
we rebuke every spirit that replaces human affection with
inordinate objects and animals.

We bind the spirit that drives the family apart because
of this behavior. Lord, we pray that You would touch the
mind. We break patterns of wrong thinking, wrong per-
ception, confusion, and double-mindedness, and we bind
spirits of schizophrenia. We rebuke deception, hiding, lethargy, and sloth in the name of the Lord.

We apply and appropriate the shed blood of Jesus
Christ over the will and break the spirit of self-will. We
break the inability to clean and discard useless items. We
break the power of laziness that leads to poverty. We bind
all tormenting and harassing spirits associated with compulsive disorders. We rebuke all repressed emotions—all

repressed anger, bitterness, rebellion, and stubbornness in Jesus's name.

Father, we pray that Your Spirit will bring wisdom, discernment, and good judgment. We loose knowledge to prevail and peace in the mind. In the name of Jesus we declare that every obsessive compulsive spirit will be destroyed from this day forward according to the power of God. We loose the spirit of humility and grace to accept the help needed to discard accumulated clutter and to release the past.

Father, we thank You for restoring the love and unity of the family that has been torn apart because of this behavior. Today let this individual choose to grow in grace and in the knowledge of our Lord and Savior Jesus Christ (2 Pet. 3:18). To You be glory both now and forever. Amen.

Chapter 5
EATING DISORDERS

Every summer my sisters and I used to visit our grandparents in Florence, Alabama. The city is known for its red clay hills, and it has a rich musical heritage. For my sisters and me, it was a wonderful place to spend our summer months.

I'll never forget one particular bright, sunny day during one of our summer visits. We were en route to the Rock Primitive Baptist Church, where my grandparents were faithful members. My grandfather served as a deacon in this church for over forty years, and my grandmother, who was known for her hearty, mouth-watering Southern dishes, served faithfully as a member of the Pastor's Aid committee.

As we were driving, I saw something unusual on the side of the road. It was a woman earnestly jogging, but I had to look again because she literally looked like a skeleton in motion. The woman was so thin her collarbones protruded from beneath her skin, and her arms looked like bones with a thin layer of skin over them. She was emaciated, and it was sad and shocking to behold.

As our car came closer to this jogger, I realized it was a young girl, maybe sixteen years old or so. She jogged fervently as though she were in a long-distance cross-country race. At the time I didn't know what to make of the situation, but now I realize that this young woman was clearly in need of a spiritual intervention.

Often we pray for the behaviors we see, but our actions stem from our thoughts, and our thoughts are rooted in our beliefs. Rather than praying for a person to stop starving or cutting herself, for instance, we need to pray against the demonic thoughts and beliefs assaulting that person's mind. The intercession for the jogger would have needed to address the way she perceived herself.

Anorexia is the loss of appetite and an inability or unwillingness to eat. Often the individual perceives herself to be fat, even though she may look perfectly fine to everyone else. Because of this false belief she doesn't eat, and she does serious damage to her body in the process. That's exactly what the enemy wants. He cometh not but for to kill, steal, and destroy (John 10:10). He uses society's unrealistic standards of the perfect body to plant seeds that distort a woman's thinking about herself, and as a result she begins down a path that destroys her health and well-being.

Bulimia is a similar disorder that also primarily affects young women, but in this case the sufferer does eat but then secretly purges by initiating vomiting. This disorder can be deadly because it damages the person's organs.

There are other young women who suffer from the same self-destructive beliefs as anorexics and bulimics but react to them in less extreme ways. They may abuse diet drugs or laxatives, or exercise excessively to achieve what they think is the perfect body. These young women may not look like skeletons walking, but they are being harassed by a vicious, tormenting spirit.

On the flip side, some people are genuinely overweight, and they are doing serious damage to their health. A person is considered obese when his weight is 20 percent or more above the ideal weight for his height. In America roughly a third of all adults are obese,[1] and they have an increased risk of diabetes, high blood pressure, and a host of other issues.

While not everyone who is overweight has an eating disorder, we are seeing Americans' waistlines get wider and

wider, and there are reasons for this. In some cases it is due
to diets filled with unhealthy fried or processed foods, or it
may be the volume of food eaten, with high-calorie snacks
and treats at every turn. Or it may be due to immobility that
prevents a person from being active.

I am acquainted with a wonderful person whose battle
with obesity began after she went to the hospital as a child
when she was suffering from an asthma attack. She was pre-
scribed medications that contained strong steroids, and the
side effect of the medicine was rapid weight gain. Because of
her severe breathing problems, she was unable to be active,
and within months of her initial treatment she began to gain
weight increasingly. Over time her battle with obesity and
immobility almost destroyed her life.

While there are physical causes for obesity, there may
be emotional causes as well. Many eating disorders can be
traced to traumatic events that led to depression and despair.
How many times have you heard of someone turning to
Häagen-Dazs after a breakup, or seeking comfort foods
when they're feeling anxious or sad?

Sadly, in our society there seems to be disdain and even
disgust toward those suffering from obesity. This kind of
hostility often causes obese individuals to isolate themselves,
which drives them further into destructive eating patterns.

Thankfully all these behaviors can be broken through
the power of prayer. I believe that through prayer individuals who have wrestled with eating disorders can experience
lasting change.

Whether we are a size 6 or a size 16, it is necessary to take
care of oneself properly. Scripture says, "What? know ye not
that your body is the temple of the Holy Ghost which is in
you, which ye have of God, and ye are not your own? For ye

are bought with a price: therefore glorify God in your body, and in your spirit, which are God's" (1 Cor. 6:19–20). It is our responsibility to glorify God in our bodies, so let's pray together for those in need of a spiritual intervention to overcome dangerous eating habits.

PRAYER FOR THOSE SUFFERING FROM EATING DISORDERS

Lord, we pray now for individuals suffering from all eating disorders—anorexia, bulimia, and obesity. We pray that Your grace will be extended to every person suffering. Lord, Your Word says, "Behold, I have graven thee upon the palms of my hands; thy walls are continually before me" (Isa. 49:16). You made us, Lord, and You know each of us by name.

For those suffering from anorexia, we pray now against every spirit that would seek to distort a person's thinking. We bind the debilitating fear of gaining weight and the fear of not being accepted because of one's size or of being considered too large. We apply and appropriate the blood of Jesus over every obsessive thought that dominates their thinking. Lord, Your Word says, "He giveth power to the faint; and to them that have no might he increaseth strength" (Isa. 40:29). So we call forth Your strength for those fighting these disorders, and we break the power of the enemy that gives them a constant distorted self-image and a false evaluation of their physical body.

For those suffering from bulimia, we arrest the desire to binge and then secretly purge the body. We come against the overuse of diuretic pills and laxatives for weight loss or to prevent weight gain. We bind self-rejection, the fear of rejection because of one's size, and the obsessive need to control weight gain in Jesus's name. We break every tormenting and harassing spirit of anxiety, apprehension, worry, and fear in Jesus's name.

Father, we pray also with compassion for the person suffering with obesity. Father, we release Your love and ask, Lord, that You give them the determination to fight for their health and their life. Deliver them from emotional eating stemming from depression, hurt, disappointment, or past trauma. We bind the spirit at the root of their overeating and the constant feeling of never being full, even after consuming the appropriate portion of food. We bind the spirit that is connected to poor nutritional habits that formed during childhood and opened the door to obesity and poor eating habits.

We break off hopelessness and life's uncontrollable disappointments. We release now, by the power of God, the spirit of true deliverance from these bondages. Father, we declare that today begins a new pattern of health, strength, and mobility in Jesus's name. We pray, Father, that You will give them healthy boundaries concerning their eating habits that will reverse years of damage.

We thank You, Lord, for empowering them to change generational cycles of unhealthy eating habits. We decree and declare a new desire for healthy foods and balanced nutrition. Most of all, we speak life and peace over them. Lord, cause them to know how much You love them. Let the words of Jeremiah 29:11 sink deep into their spirits: "For I know the thoughts that I think toward you, saith the Lord, thoughts of peace, and not of evil, to give you an expected end." In Jesus's name we pray, amen.

Chapter 6
DRUG ADDICTION

IT CAN BE a hopeless feeling to care about a person in need and feel completely powerless to help them. When a person is on a self-destructive path, often it seems that no amount of talking and reasoning does any good. It all seems to be an exercise in futility.

One of the most challenging issues for a family to deal with is drug addiction. We receive so many calls, e-mails, and Facebook messages from people seeking prayer for a loved one who is addicted to drugs. This kind of addiction has the potential to completely wreck a person's life and all who love and support him.

Sadly we've heard many news reports about celebrities who lost the battle with "their demons" when they overdosed on drugs. Whether the secular media realize it or not, they are right to say these individuals were wrestling with demonic spirits. For a drug addict, it is as though the drugs have an audible voice, calling day and night, summoning the addict to do whatever is necessary to obtain his or her drug of choice.

During these times absolutely nothing else seems to matter. A demonic spirit is at work, feeding an obsession in the mind and deep bondage in the soul. The addict's every thought competes with the longing to experience the temporary satisfaction of a high.

Let's take a closer look at addiction. Except in cases of overdose, drugs destroy a person gradually. It turns vibrant, healthy, attractive people into emaciated, broken, lost individuals. It can be amazing to see the dramatic way drug abuse can transform a person's physical appearance.

Drug abuse can damage brain cells, causing slow and slurred speech. Addicts can lose their hair and teeth as well as significant amounts of weight. In the case of those who inject drugs using needles, the constant stress can create bruises at the injection sites and even cause their veins to collapse.

Many who snort cocaine damage their nasal septum, resulting in constant sniffing and a never-ending runny nose. The effects are not only physical. Drug addicts may also have episodes of paranoia, delusional visions, and an exaggerated sense of self-importance. You can often hear this in their conversation.

In the movies we see images of the addict who lives for the next high. He has lost his home, his job, and his family, and he walks around in tattered clothes, doing almost anything to get money for another high. Yet not all drug addicts look that way. There are functioning drug addicts who are often able to deceive everyone around them into thinking nothing is wrong. However, this deception can last only for so long.

As the bondage grows in the addict, it becomes more obvious that he really isn't in control. No matter how hard he tries to hide the symptoms of his addiction, even a novice will be able to recognize the increasing nervousness, anxiety, and shakiness as signs that something is wrong.

It is incredibly painful to observe the gradual change in personality—the loss of laughter, the undeniable sadness, and the constant suspicion. But as painful as this progression is to watch, typically it is only when a person has hit rock bottom that he begins to consider getting help.

How do you pray for a person who is on this path of self-destruction? Addiction may be formidable, but, child of

God, you are neither powerless nor helpless. The power of prayer overcomes bondage and breaks shackles of every kind. Yes, everyone has a will, but the Bible says the heart of the king is in God's hands. That means we can pray for the Holy Spirit to touch a person's mind and heart and give him the desire to change.

As believers we are seated with Christ, far above all principality, power, and every work of the adversary. That means we can speak boldly to the demonic forces seeking to destroy those bound by drug addiction. Jesus declared, "Verily I say unto you, Whatsoever ye shall bind on earth shall be bound in heaven: and whatsoever ye shall loose on earth shall be loosed in heaven" (Matt. 18:18). That is not only for a select few; that is for all of us who have called upon the name of the Lord unto salvation.

We overcome by the blood of the Lamb and by the word of our testimony. The Bible says, "And having spoiled principalities and powers, he made a shew of them openly, triumphing over them in it" (Col. 2:15). We don't need to fear the enemy. Jesus triumphed over him on the cross, and because of the blood He shed, we can declare His victory over every demonic stronghold. Hallelujah!

As saints of God we are seated with Christ in heavenly places far above all principalities and powers (Eph. 1:20; 2:6). That means we have been given authority over every demonic spirit. We must use this authority in prayer and fervent intercession. *Fervent* means "to boil with intensity." If a loved one is addicted to drugs, it is no time to be passive in the battle. Let us declare war on these demonic strongholds and claim the victory.

PRAYER FOR A DRUG ADDICT

Heavenly Father, we thank You for the dominion and authority given to every believer through the power of the blood of Jesus. Father, we pray now for the addicted person, first that You would shower him/her with the pure agape love of Jesus Christ. We break all spirits of low self-esteem, low self-worth, rejection, and disappointment. Holy Spirit, we ask that You surround him/her with Your presence and give him/her strength to receive deliverance and begin recovery.

We take dominion over every form of substance abuse. We break the power of addictions of every kind. We arrest the cravings and yearning for temporary satisfaction. Father, we bind the spirit of selfishness, every lying spirit, and every strongman connected to drug abuse. We apply the blood of Jesus to the mind, the brain cells, the veins, and every entrance and gateway utilized during drug use. We speak now to the voice of the drug that calls them; we apply and appropriate the powerful shed blood of Jesus to deny the enemy access to the mind. We pray against the spirit that awakens them out of their sleep craving drugs. The blood of Jesus prevails.

We come against spirits of nervousness, anxiety, fear, helplessness, hopelessness, and depression. We come against every driving spirit that leads a person back to drugs. We sever all ties with drug dealers through obligation, fear, and all forms of control.

We arrest the spirit that tells the addict, "You just can't break free." We bind the lies and deceit of the enemy. Lord, empower them with Your Word and set them free. We come against the spirit of dishonesty and denial, and we humbly ask, Lord, that You help them to stop running and surrender to You this day. Lord, we thank You for releasing the power of breakthrough as we pray together now in Your great name.

Lord, we drive out every spirit connected to cocaine, methamphetamines, barbiturates, Ecstasy, heroine, pain-killers, and morphine abuse. In the name of Jesus we break the bondage of all over-the-counter medicines that are currently being abused. We speak to wills and emotions and the thinking that "God has given me freedom and I deserve to be happy and free." Holy Spirit, we ask that You purge their system and cleanse them of every trace of the addiction, in the name of Jesus.

Father, we speak to the soul to be completely delivered from this stronghold and never, ever return to it, in the matchless name of Jesus. For the temple of God is holy, which temple we are (1 Cor. 3:17). Lord, I praise You that this deliverance will not be partial, but complete, and they will experience complete freedom from every bondage mentioned in this prayer for Your glory, Lord.

In Jesus's name, now, Lord, fill every void, heal every broken place, and set the captives totally and completely free according to Your Word. We are confident of this very thing, that He which hath begun a good work will perform it until the day of Jesus Christ (Phil. 1:6). In Jesus's name, amen.

If you have been delivered of addiction or want to reaffirm the freedom you have because of the shed blood of Jesus, I encourage you to pray the following prayer:

Declaration of the
Covenant of the Blood

Through the blood of Jesus I am redeemed out of the hand of the devil. Through the blood of Jesus all my sins are forgiven. The blood of Jesus Christ, God's Son, is cleansing me now from all sin. Through the blood of Jesus I am justified, which means I've been made righteous, just as if I had never sinned. Through the blood of Jesus I am sanctified, made holy, and set apart for God. My body is the temple of the Holy Spirit; it is redeemed and cleansed by the blood of Jesus. I belong to the Lord Jesus Christ, God's Son, body, soul, and spirit. His blood protects me from all evil. Because of the blood of Jesus Satan has no more power over me and no more place in me. I renounce him and his hosts completely and declare them to be my enemies. Jesus said, "These signs shall follow believers, in my name shall they cast out devils." I am a believer, and in the name of Jesus Christ I exercise my authority and expel all evil spirits. I command them to leave me now, according to the Word of God.

We overcome by the blood of the Lamb and by the word of our testimony. I declare that I am an overcomer, because I am washed in the blood of the Lord Jesus Christ. Hallelujah!

Spiritual Intervention for Families and Relationships

Chapter 7
FAMILY DYSFUNCTION

T HE ENEMY HATES the family, first because God established the family before the church, and second because Satan has neither father nor mother, neither sister nor brother. He is a fallen angel and was rejected from the presence of God. His family consists of fallen demonic spirits that were violently cast out of heaven with him.

You can choose your friends, the select group of individuals who become part of your inner social circle, but the truth is, you don't choose your family. You're born into a particular group of people. We are all strategically placed into the world by design and have no control over the family of which we become a member.

It is wonderful to be raised in a home that is radiating with love and support, where family members genuinely respect and love one another. Unfortunately, not all families are that way. Many families are considered dysfunctional because they are in constant conflict, continuously behaving in inappropriate ways or acting outside of social norms.

Every family has disagreements at one point or another, but for some people those conflicts are more of a lifelong struggle. Their home life is filled with family confusion, disrespect, and emotional pain.

Some families are completely torn apart because of poor communication; others are in crisis because of constant bickering. In some cases there is tension among family members because some within the family are constantly attempting to gain control.

Destructive patterns form as family members fail to

work together and communicate their needs and desires in a respectful and healthy way. Disrespect and discourtesy can play a very big part in family conflict. Something as simple as not honoring a person's time and space can compound the ongoing problems.

Add to that the fact that there are such things as generational curses. Some family problems can be traced back several generations. Until the pattern is broken, the same destructive behavior will keep manifesting itself in a family.

There are many examples of dysfunctional families in the Bible. Joseph's family is one such case. Born to Jacob and Rachel, Joseph was surrounded by a host of siblings, including eleven brothers. Each brother had a distinct personality and was known for his behavior. Take, for instance, his older brother Reuben. Scripture tells us he was as unstable as water (Gen. 49:4).

Joseph was a dreamer and was beloved and highly favored by his parents. The Bible says Joseph's father made him a coat of many colors. This created unthinkable tension; a deep, seething spirit of anger, jealousy, and even murder began to burn in the hearts of a few of Joseph's brothers. They began plotting to kill him but changed their minds at the last minute and decided instead to sell him into slavery. Talk about brotherly love!

The Bible teaches that "love is strong as death; jealousy is cruel as the grave: the coals thereof are coals of fire, which hath a most vehement flame" (Song of Sol. 8:6). Jealousy causes people to endlessly compare themselves to one another, and it can affect the sense of love and unity among family members. Jealousy drives unhealthy competition. It causes people to find their worth in their accomplishments and discredit those who have not achieved similar results.

Jealousy is a combination of inadequacy, resentment, and anger. It can't stand to see a rival—or anyone, for that matter—enjoying success or having an advantage. Caused by a lack of self-confidence and a poor self-image, jealousy feeds deep negative thoughts and feelings born out of insecurity, fear, and anxiety over an anticipated loss of something that a person values.

Just as in the story of Joseph, not only can a family member's jealousy create tension within the home, but it can also lead to deeply hurtful actions. But as I said previously, you can't choose your family, and oftentimes you can't just walk away from those relationships, even in adulthood. And even if you could walk away, you may not want to; Joseph loved his brothers despite all the pain he endured because of their actions. So how do you love your family members in the midst of dysfunction?

Separate the Two

My mother, Dr. Angie Ray, helped many people achieve personal freedom with a simple but powerful principle. She taught us to "separate the two": love the person or family member but understand that they are being influenced by a spirit. Love the person; hate the sin. If you can separate the actions from the person, it will help you identify the motivation behind his behavior. You will discover the spirit behind his actions.

When it comes to dysfunctional family members, you must forgive them and seek to discern the spirit influencing their behavior. We only hurt ourselves when we refuse to forgive and dwell on the offense, thinking that by holding on to our anger we are somehow punishing the other person. When we hold on to bitterness and unforgiveness, we grieve the Holy Spirit and block the hand of God from moving in our life. Scripture says:

> And grieve not the holy Spirit of God, whereby ye are sealed unto the day of redemption. Let all bitterness, and wrath, and anger, and clamour, and evil speaking, be put away from you, with all malice: and be ye kind one to another, tenderhearted, forgiving one another, even as God for Christ's sake hath forgiven you.
>
> —EPHESIANS 4:30–32

This is what Joseph decided to do. He chose to forgive despite the pain his brothers' actions caused.

> So shall ye say unto Joseph, Forgive, I pray thee now, the trespass of thy brethren, and their sin; for they did unto thee evil: and now, we pray thee, forgive the trespass of the servants of the God of thy father. And Joseph wept when they spake unto him. And his brethren also went and fell down before his face; and they said, Behold, we be thy servants. And Joseph said unto them, Fear not: for am I in the place of God? But as for you, ye thought evil against me; but God meant it unto good, to bring to pass, as it is this day, to save much people alive.
>
> —GENESIS 50:17–20

As you can see in the passage above, Joseph had the wisdom to discern what was happening spiritually behind the scenes. What his brothers meant for harm, God meant for good. God used the pain and dysfunction to bring about His purposes in Joseph's life. He will do the same for you and me. He causes all things, even family dysfunction, to work together for good to them that love God and who are the called according to His purpose (Rom. 8:28).

God desires for families to be rooted and grounded in love (Eph. 3:17). Being rooted in love is being willing to embrace and exemplify unconditional respect. Respect proceeds love. My parents taught my sisters and me a simple message that kept us rooted in love and helped us during critical times. It is simply that "we are stronger together, so we must stick together."

Let's agree together in prayer for our family relationships:

Prayer for Dysfunctional Families

Loving heavenly Father, we come to You at this time asking for wisdom for families who are suffering from dysfunction and disunity. We humbly ask for wisdom to address the root of the problems that keep resurfacing during family interactions. We pray that You show us what is at the root of the repetitive arguments and family anger, and that You minister emotional healing to those who are bruised from years of dysfunctional conduct.

We address every destructive cycle that brings division, contention, and strife into the family. We bind every passive spirit and every aggressive spirit. We bind the cycle of domestic violence and every spirit that is acting out through loved ones who are hurt, angry, and disappointed. We bind all rebellion and uncontrollable behavior. We break the power of all wrong perceptions, false judgments, and emotional reactions that keep past hurts alive.

We ask, Father, that the spirit of love, forgiveness, and true parental nurturing fill every void in Jesus's name. We bind the patterns of anger, intolerance, and escapism to cope with family stress. We come against bloodline assignments that have traveled through the bloodline for decades.

Lord, Your Word says that You know the plans You have for us, plans to prosper us and not harm us, plans to give us hope and a future (Jer. 29:11). I thank You for family restoration this day in the name of Jesus Christ, and I pray that this family be rooted and grounded in love, according to Ephesians 3:14–21. I ask that they would be able to comprehend what is the breadth, and length, and depth, and height; and to know the love of Christ, which passeth knowledge, that they might be filled with all the fullness of God. Now unto You who are able to do exceeding abundantly above all that we ask or think, according to the power that worketh in us. To You be glory throughout all ages, world without end, in the matchless name of Jesus. Amen.

Chapter 8
SINGLE WOMEN

Today as the percentage of single women continues to grow, so do the questions. "Lord, You said You would give me the desires of my heart. Why am I still single?"

It seems that singleness to some is like an invisible cloud that denotes a sense of failure. It is like some type of plague. In our society it seems that a cloak of negativity blankets those who are not in relationships. Even at church so much emphasis is put on strengthening marriages and families—which is needed—that many singles are left feeling like something's missing until they are married and have a family of their own. It is like they're in a holding pattern, walking around with question marks over their heads.

As a single woman, I write this chapter from a place of surety. I praise the Lord that, whether married or single, "I am fearfully and wonderfully made: marvellous are [His] works; and that my soul knoweth right well" (Ps. 139:14). But I understand how a lot of single women feel when people ask, "Are you married?" or, "When will you get married?" In their defense I would like to mention a few obvious reasons for the increased number of singles today.

First, many people have unrealistic expectations of relationships. In our fast-paced society women are constantly bombarded with images of perfection on TV and in movies, in magazines, and even on Facebook, Twitter, and Instagram. Thinking this is what it takes to attract a suitable, available mate, women are driven to be the prettiest, wealthiest, most active person around. Some are resorting to plastic surgery to get the perfect figure, as if they are in some type of competition to achieve the perfect body.

Perfect looks won't bring the perfect man or lead to a perfect marriage. God has given each of us everything we need to accomplish His will for our lives. That means the person He has for you will find you attractive without any nips or tucks. And every marriage goes through difficult times. That's why the Bible tells us to delight ourselves in the Lord and not in a spouse. He's the only one who can truly satisfy the longings of our hearts.

Second, there has been a spiritual attack on men and godly manhood. We cannot ignore the painful reality that many men of marrying age are, for whatever reason, unavailable. Disproportionate numbers of African American and Hispanic men are incarcerated, and a growing number of men are choosing alternative lifestyles. Some men are openly gay while others are bisexual and keep their same-sex relationships and confusion about their sexual identity a secret. By doing so, they expose a potential wife to emotional devastation and sexually transmitted diseases.

Please don't get me wrong; I have the utmost love, honor, and respect for men. Men are made in the image of God. There are secure, handsome, mighty men of God who want to get married. I am simply being honest about the plight of many single women who face a shrinking pool of eligible, God-fearing potential mates.

This brings us to another group I call the "playas." These men are in a category unto themselves. They are acutely aware of the deficit of eligible men, and because of it they consider themselves a type of commodity. Typically these men date several women simultaneously without even the slightest concern for the hurt they may cause. They freely use women for personal gain as a type of resource, allowing women to buy everything for them, from cell phones to Bentleys and Maseratis.

They have systematically mastered the art of seduction by saying precisely what women want to hear. The playa knows how to keep single women waiting for the thing they tend to want most: a commitment. Often playas masterfully lead women on year after year, using false hope of a future together as bait to keep them waiting. They give just enough hope to keep women under their control. The problem is that playas give this same hope to multiple women simultaneously, often in different locations and even cities.

For a playa a commitment is the potential loss of multiple streams of income from other hopeful women. They don't want to commit to one woman because that requires ending relationships that will cut off his benefits

These playas are operating under what I call a spirit of Casanova. The goal of this spirit is to seduce and charm single women by captivating them with words they long to hear. Idealism and romanticism can cloud the judgment of single women. The image of the white wedding dress and the white picket fence surrounding the beautiful home play in many women's minds like a matinee. Driven by the longing for a family and children against the backdrop of a ticking biological clock, a woman can find herself settling for the wrong man and tolerating unacceptable behavior. It's heart-wrenching to watch women endure mistreatment and waste precious time waiting for proposals that will never come.

"Eeny, meeny, miny, moe" is the new male dilemma, brought on by the great number of available, attractive women. Casanova is like a kid in a candy store, turning around and around in circles, searching but unable to choose and commit to one. This spirit is not simply indecisive; it is devious as it strings several women along, all of them unaware of the other women he is seeing at the same time.

It amazes me to watch this Casanova spirit at work. It feeds off the idea that a woman is lacking something if she is unmarried. Scripture tells us that we are complete in Him, whether married or not (Col. 2:10). Many single women today are financially independent and are accomplished in their careers. They are talented and intelligent, yet they think they are somehow lacking. I thank God that there are polished and intelligent Christian women who have self-respect, moral values, and godly standards. As Proverbs 31:25 says, "Strength and honour are her clothing; and she shall rejoice in time to come." Those are the very attributes the enemy wants to steal from single women.

It is a plan of the enemy to give the impression that being a saved, single Christian is a miserable existence. Don't believe the lie. I can honestly say it is an enormous joy serving God and reaching humanity as a single person. The Bible tells us there are benefits to being single. As the apostle Paul states, the unmarried woman is free to care for the things of God (1 Cor. 7:34). It is true that there is a group of singles who find genuine fulfillment in the work of ministry, but no matter what state we find ourselves in, married or single, we are to be content (Phil. 4:11).

For those who desire to marry and are wondering when God will bring them a mate, please know this: God loves you, and He made a man of God for you who will not play games with your emotions. He will honor, love, and respect you. Don't settle.

Isaiah was a true prophet. It is as though he lived in our day and time. He prophesied, "And in that day seven women shall take hold of one man, saying, We will eat our own bread, and wear our own apparel: only let us be called by thy name, to take away our reproach" (Isa. 4:1). Because of the imbalance in the ratio of Christian single women to Christian single men, there seems to be an increase in the spirit of disappointment that leads to desperation, especially among women who feel they have a limited time to start a family.

The Bible says, "For of this sort are they which creep into houses, and lead captive silly women laden with sins, led away with divers lusts" (2 Tim. 3:6). "What is a silly woman?" you may ask. The word *silly* in the Greek means "a little woman," which indicates a woman who lacks self-respect. It is also defined as a woman who is "weak-willed." A weak-willed woman, according to the scripture, is a gullible woman. To be gullible simply means to be easily deceived or cheated. Gullible women have a tendency to believe everything men say without question. Silly women have a very difficult time resisting the captivating words of lustful and lascivious men. Many fall prey to the spirit of lust because of their inability to take a stand.

The assignment of the enemy is to make the godly single woman succumb to the pressure to get involved emotionally (and physically) with someone who is not God's choice for her. Watch the setup: the enemy brings discouragement over a woman's single state. Feeling sorry for herself, she begins to date someone who does not love God or who is not committed to following His Word. She thinks God won't satisfy the desires of her heart, so she gives her heart to someone God never wanted in her life in the first place. She may even fall into sexual sin, which is a sin not only against God but also against her own body.

The enemy is cunning, and he will use any opening to get

us off track. Don't be discouraged. If you have found yourself in bad relationships in the past, perhaps with a playa, don't allow bitterness to get into your heart. Remember, all things work together for good to them that love God and who are called according to His purpose (Rom. 8:28). Every experience has a purpose. It was not just for you. There are some trials God allowed you to go through so you would be able to help someone else who is facing the same test. Embrace the lessons you have learned during the painful seasons of your life. If you've fallen into the trap of the enemy and gotten involved with the wrong man, repent, forgive those who have hurt you, and forgive yourself. Then move forward. Scripture says God has good plans for us (Jer. 29:11). That is true even if you have made mistakes.

Commit Your Ways to the Lord

God has given us many promises in His Word, and they are true. The Bible says, "Delight thyself also in the LORD; and he shall give thee the desires of thine heart. Commit thy way unto the LORD; trust also in him; and he shall bring it to pass" (Ps. 37:4–5).

As born-again believers we must put our faith in God no matter what the circumstances look like. Everything God has planned for us from the foundation of the earth will come to pass, including marriage, in His timing. Be encouraged. Don't let the enemy overwhelm you with fear, rejection, or hopelessness. Focus on God and trust His plan for you. His Word is more reliable than any dating book on the best seller list.

The Bible says, "For in him we live, and move, and have our being" (Acts 17:28). *Trust and wait on God!* "They that wait upon the LORD shall renew their strength" (Isa. 40:31).

One final note to my single sisters: the Scriptures declare, "Whoso findeth a wife findeth a good thing, and obtaineth favour of the LORD" (Prov. 18:22). The woman has a decision in the matter, of course, but the precedent has been set that the man should find a wife, not that the woman find a husband. God put Adam to sleep and created a woman from his rib. He also knows whom you need in your life and when that person should come. Keep an optimistic outlook, stay joyful, and know that the best is yet to come.

Prayer for Single Women

Lord, we bring all the single women to the altar in Your presence. We pray a special prayer for single women who love You, Lord. Father, You know them name by name. We ask You, Lord, to envelop them with Your agape love.

We intercede now for women who are in need of direction, instruction, and strength. Lord, we know You made every woman to receive genuine love and affection. Lord, Your Word says that "the unmarried woman careth for the things of the Lord, that she may be holy both in body and in spirit" (1 Cor. 7:34). Father, help these single sisters to care for the things that bring glory to You, and teach them to honor You by walking in holiness in body and in spirit.

We pray that You will cause them to know that they are not failures because of their single status. We pray against every spirit of rejection, self-rejection, and fear of rejection in the lives of these women. We bind the hurt and disappointment they feel. We arrest every spirit causing physical suffering, emotional anguish, and hopelessness in the name of Jesus. We break the power of deep hurt from years invested in broken relationships.

We come against every spirit of seduction and lust and all charming and alluring spirits in Jesus's name. We release now the spirit of love and healing in the area of the soul.

We bind every spirit of mind control, commandeering spirit, familiar spirit, and seducing spirit. We break every stronghold of false hope from over the mind in Jesus's name. We rebuke the feeling of desperation because of time gone by, and all despondency and hopelessness. We rebuke every demonic attempt to pressure these women to lower their moral standards and Christian values in an effort to attract or keep a partner.

Father, give them the wisdom and courage of Ruth and the virtue and strength of Esther as they wait for Your divine and perfect will. We thank You, Lord, that Your Word declares that we are to delight ourselves in You and You will give us the desires of our hearts (Ps. 37:4).

We thank You, Lord, for wholeness through You. We thank You for genuine happiness and abundant joy. We are complete in You, the head of all principality and power (Col. 2:10).

Father, we declare and decree honorable and holy marriages that will bring glory to You. Lord, we know that You have a remnant unto Yourself. Father, bless the mighty men of purpose and valor. We pray that You will speak to them and lead them to the wives You would have them to marry. Keep them from the snare of the enemy, and bless them financially to be a blessing to a family in the name of Jesus.

Lord, we commit to set our affections on things above, not on things on the earth (Col. 3:2). All this we pray in the matchless name of Jesus. Amen.

Chapter 9
PROTECTION FOR CHILDREN

I T WAS A Sunday morning I will never forget. Our ministry was having our weekly services in an old theater on the South Side of Chicago. There was something so special about our church services; they were always so liberating, anointed, and joyful. I remember the sound that filled the sanctuary—the richness of the Hammond B3 organ, the splendid depth of the bass guitar, the rhythmic snap of the snare drum, and the crash of the cymbals.

On this particular day, as I was preparing to leave service after a wonderful time in worship, a four-year-old girl came to me with an exuberant smile and warm disposition. She said, "Sister Kim, I am praying for you." It is difficult to put into words the joy I felt at that moment. Her words came from such a pure place. I was moved and uplifted by the fact that this little girl was praying for me. I was struck by her pure love and innocence, and somehow I knew that God would honor her request.

Children have an innocence that is so special to God. Throughout Scripture God has used children in powerful ways. God chose Samuel to be His prophet when he was still a young child, and the Lord blessed David to tend his father's sheep as a boy. He chose Josiah to become a king at the age of eight, and Josiah reigned for thirty-one years.

I had to include a chapter in this book for children because, regretfully, times have changed drastically for children. There was a time when children could grow up carefree. Now they must be informed at an early age about predators. I pray that God will give parents great discernment about the people who are around their children and that they will take action when something needs to be addressed.

It is easy for parents to become fearful for their children and family members with all the horror stories on the news. But the Lord gives us a promise in His Word: "Because thou hast made the LORD, which is my refuge, even the most High, thy habitation; there shall no evil befall thee, neither shall any plague come nigh thy dwelling. For he shall give his angels charge over thee, to keep thee in all thy ways" (Ps. 91:9–11). In this passage the Lord is promising to protect not only us but also our "dwelling," or our house.

Psalm 112:7 tells us that if our hearts are fixed on the Lord, trusting in Him, we will not be afraid of evil tidings. When our hearts are steadfast, trusting in God's promises, we will not live in constant fear that harm will come to our children. Scripture says God "wilt keep him in perfect peace, whose mind is stayed on thee: because he trusteth in thee" (Isa. 26:3).

God is omnipresent; that means He is present everywhere all the time. God is able to be where the parents cannot be, to shield and protect children from hurt, harm, and danger. God doesn't want us to live in fear, but to faithfully trust Him to protect our children and families.

PRAYER FOR CHILDREN

Precious Lord, we praise You for Your children. Father, we thank You for Your powerful hand of protection. We humbly ask that You allow Your wonderful presence to shadow every child. We ask that You send Your angels to protect them daily.

We ask You to teach them Your ways and help them to have an obedient spirit to obey their parents and teachers.

We pray that they will grow in grace and knowledge with kindness and love. We ask You to shield and protect them from every predator; give them a watchful eye and an understanding to know when something is not right. Lord, we ask that You reveal every plot and plan of the enemy concerning them.

We come against mass shootings, gang violence, and murder, in the name of Jesus. Lead Your children in the opposite direction when there is imminent danger. We war against the spirit of molestation. We bind all tormenting fear that will cause silence when mistreatment occurs. Lord, give children the presence of mind to inform an adult when they are threatened, bullied, or abused. We break every perverse design and plan to decide their sexuality. We pray, Father, that You will expose every plan to seduce or abuse them sexually, in the name of Jesus.

I ask, Lord, that You will give their parents great wisdom, discernment, and insight. Teach parents to raise their children up in the fear and admonition of the Lord and to cultivate their children's gifts and talents so that they may bring glory to God. I thank You, Lord, for giving children an excellent spirit in the area of their education. Let them excel in their goals and endeavors and lay hold of the great future You desire for them.

I loose the joy, happiness, and laughter that children should experience. Let them know, Father, that You created them and that You love them.

We are instructed to pray after this manner: "Our Father which art in heaven, hallowed be thy name. Thy kingdom come, Thy will be done in earth, as it is in heaven. Give us this day our daily bread. And forgive us our debts, as we forgive our debtors. And lead us not *into temptation, but deliver us from evil: for Thine is the kingdom, and the power, and the glory, for ever. Amen." We know Your Word says that if we forgive others their trespasses, You will also forgive us. But if we do not forgive others, neither will You forgive us (Matt. 6:9–15). So we release to You those who have wronged us. We honor You and trust that You hear our prayer and will answer. In Jesus's name, amen.*

Special Prayer for Pastors' Children

Dear heavenly Father, hear our cry, O God, and let Your ear be attentive today (Ps. 61:1–3) as we lift up the children of pastors and ministers. Lord, so often they are misunderstood and expected to be completely perfect in the eyes of the congregation. Father, I humbly ask that You free them from all pain caused by unrealistic expectations, their family members, or the church.

We come against all hurt and disappointment because of the feeling that they were not always a priority. We address all repressed anger, resentment, or hurt because of the time their parents spent at church, meetings, hospitals, funerals, and away from the family. We break down walls of deep hurt and neglect.

We bind all hurt caused by members of the church, any wounds resulting from spoken words, and all pain stemming from attitudes or actions that were insensitive and cruel. We place the blood of Jesus upon the souls of these children and ask for healing and complete freedom.

We break the power of rebellion that seeks to establish its own identity within ministers' children and cause them to do the opposite of what their parents have taught them.

Lord, we break all spirits of defiance and rebellion that lead to backsliding in an effort to be seen and heard as an individual and to establish their own identity and personality. We ask, Lord, that You would lead them not into temptation but deliver them from evil.

Father, give pastors' children hearts of love, forgiveness, and understanding. Allow every painful test to become a powerful testimony. In the precious name of Jesus we speak life. Amen.

Special Prayer for Military Families

Father, today we pray for families of members of the armed forces. Lord, Your Word says the steps of a good man are ordered by the Lord. We ask that You go before these military families and give them favor as they transition to a new area. We ask for the grace to meet every challenge with optimism, and we pray that the relocation will be a time for positive personal growth and exciting change. Lord, we pray for Your provision in every area—adequate schools for the children, jobs for those seeking employment, and fulfillment for those who are seeking direction.

Lord, we pray for military veterans and soldiers who have faithfully served their country and suffered injuries during their time in the service. Father, we ask for healing for post-traumatic stress disorder (PTSD). Touch the area of the mind that causes painful memory recall and images that disrupt their sleep. We pray against all mental trauma and forms of escapism. We pray for peace in the mind, recovery, and restoration.

Lord, we ask for supernatural increase for those who are serving or have served in the armed forces. Lord, we ask that You bless them with adequate housing for their families. Bless their children with scholarships and finances to attend college and become successful in the vocation they choose.

We also speak protection to those men and women serving abroad, that You shield them from hurt, harm, and danger, and we ask that You send angels to surround their loved ones back home. We pray all these things in the all-powerful name of Your Son, Jesus. Amen.

Chapter 10
HEALING AFTER DIVORCE

DIVORCE HAS OFTEN been compared to death itself. With divorce often comes the loss of certain hopes, dreams, and promises, and facing those losses is not easy. Those going through divorce often describe immense pain and heartache. Some have shared with me that it felt like their hearts were literally breaking, while others expressed intense anger and unforgiveness.

Unforgiveness is a dangerous emotion. It can lead to bitterness, which may produce hostility and a desire to retaliate against those we believe have wronged us. Though bitterness may stem from severe pain caused by someone else's wrongdoing, it produces very bad fruit that can do us great harm. That is why Hebrews 12:15 warns us to not let any bitter root spring up and trouble us. Holding on to bitterness after divorce can harm a person's bond with their children, their parents or former in-laws, and even their future relationships.

For some who have gone through divorce, shame looms overhead like a cloud. They become preoccupied with what others think of them, and they may become tormented by regret. I have prayed with many people who cannot forgive themselves after going through divorce. They ask over and over, "What could I have done differently? What did I do wrong?" They are trying to find a logical explanation for why their marriages did not work.

We must realize that the devil is looking for ways to put us in bondage. By wallowing in self-condemnation and shame, a person may unwittingly fall prey to a spirit of rejection, which can be an insidious spirit. Those oppressed by rejection may begin to feel unworthy or that no one cares about them anymore. They may think they can't do anything right or that they are utter failures. This mind-set just puts them in further bondage.

There are many causes for divorce. Physical or emotional unfaithfulness is a common cause, but in our ministry we are seeing more and more people who are dealing with psychological abuse and mental cruelty. We are encountering this so much that I am devoting an entire chapter of this book to addressing that issue. The emotional trauma that results from psychological abuse erodes self-worth and eventually breaks the spirit. This leaves abuse victims with a need for healing from both the pain of divorce and the emotional scars left from the abuse.

Even if unfaithfulness or abuse was the reason the marriage ended, that doesn't necessarily lessen the pain, especially when children are involved. Divorce affects everyone who cares about both parties. Close friends and family may feel torn, as though they must choose one party or the other. This may compound feelings of guilt, which the enemy may use to heap condemnation on those who are already blaming themselves.

Divorce grieves the heart of God because He created marriage to reflect His covenant with us, His bride. Yet He gave each of us a free will, and He does not want to see His children suffer in abusive situations. No matter what we have been through, He will never leave us or forsake us. The Lord is always faithful. He came to heal the brokenhearted and to set the oppressed free.

If you are facing a divorce or have gone through divorce, the Holy Spirit is able to meet you where you are and minister His healing power to every broken place. The following prayer is written for those who need healing after divorce. I am standing in agreement for freedom and peace, but the divorced individual must be willing to release any unforgiveness and bitterness in order to walk in the freedom he or she has in Christ. For that reason some of the prayer is written for the divorcee to declare over his or her situation, and I included a prayer of forgiveness.

It is God's will for us to enter into His rest, which can be very hard for someone whose finances, emotions, and family have been shattered by divorce. That is why I also have included a declaration of peace at the end of this chapter. Those who have experienced divorce or other emotional trauma can declare this truth and expect God to bring supernatural peace and rest.

Prayer for Healing After Divorce

Father, Your Word declares that when we stand praying, we must forgive if we have ought against any, that our Father in heaven may forgive us our trespasses (Mark 11:25). So we pray that as an act of his/her will, [insert name] will choose to forgive every offense, disappointment, and deep hurt resulting from a failed marriage. (See prayer of forgiveness below.) Empower him/her to choose to "let all bitterness, and wrath, and anger, and clamour, and evil speaking, be put away from [me], with all malice: and [to be] kind one to another, tenderhearted, forgiving one another, even as God for Christ's sake hath forgiven [me]" (Eph. 4:31–32).

We pray that he/she will give up all hostility toward any person who was directly or indirectly involved in the dissolution of the marriage. Let him/her forgive all in-laws and relatives in the name of Jesus.

Father, we know that You hate divorce, but You gave every person a free will. We ask You, Lord, for closure and the wisdom to accept what You allow. We pray, Lord, that You will heal the emotional tear, the pain, and the heartache. Lord, we ask for emotional stability and the strength to move forward with hopeful expectation in the name of Jesus.

We bind all spirits of anger, rage, and retaliation. We bind every mind-binding, tormenting, or harassing spirit that would attempt to gain access. We bind any spirit that entered in during this time and that may be holding open a door for the enemy to attack. We come against every spirit that entered through emotional abuse, psychological anguish, or mental cruelty. And we release peace where there has been confusion and the oil of joy where there have been tears and hurt.

Lord, we thank You for giving us the courage to accept the things we cannot change and the wisdom to know the difference. We apply the blood of Jesus to every area affected in body and soul by the divorce. Father, we ask You for an anointing that brings supernatural healing and emotional wellness.

We break all remaining spirits of depression and every satanic attempt to bring bondage. We break all spirits of heaviness, pain, and hurt this day in the precious name of Jesus. Give Your child wisdom to communicate with civility and kindness. We thank You for also healing the children, relatives, and friends who have been affected by the divorce.

We thank You, Lord, that You will not allow more than we can bear. We are confident that You will restore Your precious child's soul and bring joy into his/her life *again. We thank You for giving him/her strength and the determination to take one day at a time. We declare and decree that today begins a new day. [Name individual] will live again and have joy. Life is not over.*

Father, teach Your child how to walk in total freedom. We trust Your Word that says, "A new heart also will I give you, and a new spirit will I put within you: and I will take away the stony heart out of your flesh, and I will give you an heart of flesh" (Ezek. 36:26). This we pray in the matchless name of Jesus. Amen.

PRAYER OF FORGIVENESS

Lord, I have a confession to make: At times I have resented certain people who have hurt and disappointed me. I have held unforgiveness in my heart toward them, and I call upon You to help me to forgive them. I now forgive [name the individual, whether living or dead] and ask You to forgive them also, and bless them in the name of Jesus Christ. Amen.

A DECLARATION OF PEACE

Lord, I cast all of my cares upon You for You care for me. I know that You love me, and I love You. You said, "Come unto me, all ye that labour and are heavy laden, and I will give you rest" (Matt. 11:28). Lord Jesus, I come to You. I bring my past, present, and future. I bring to You [name the person, place, or thing] and every other situation or set of circumstances that concern me. Lord Jesus, I am giving all of these cares and burdens to You, and I leave them with You.

Lord, You said in Your Word that for the people of God there is a rest. Lord, take my hand and lead me into that rest. I thank You for Your love and peace that surpasses all understanding. I speak these words in the power and authority of the Holy Ghost, and I bind and cast out every hindering spirit of doubt and unbelief, in Jesus's name. You are my peace, and I will remain in Your peace because I will keep my mind on You (Isa. 26:3). I declare right now that Your peace will rule in my heart and in this situation, in Jesus's name. Amen.

Spiritual Intervention for Health and Healing

Chapter 11
PHYSICAL ILLNESS

T HERE ARE FEW feelings worse than being called into your doctor's office and given a negative report. In that moment everything seems to go into a tailspin, but in times like those we have a critical choice to make.

The Bible tells us to "be careful for nothing; but in every thing by prayer and supplication with thanksgiving let your requests be made known unto God. And the peace of God, which passeth all understanding, shall keep your hearts and minds through Christ Jesus" (Phil. 4:6–7). When faced with unexpected bad news, we must stop and make a decision. We must decide whether to give in to fear and anxiety, or to take dominion over our thoughts.

The enemy will seek to magnify the negative. If the doctor says there's a lump, the enemy will tell you it's an inoperable tumor. If the doctor says there's a shadow on your lung, the enemy will tell you it's cancer. The enemy will have you planning your funeral if you let him.

This is why you must cast down imaginations and declare God's Word over the situation. You must cast down every high thing that exalts itself against the knowledge of God and bring into captivity the thoughts that are contrary to God's Word (2 Cor. 10:4–5). The battle for our thoughts is a spiritual war, and we must use spiritual weapons to fight it.

Ephesians 6 tells us to "put on the whole armour of God, that ye may be able to stand against the wiles of the devil. For we wrestle not against flesh and blood, but against principalities, against powers, against the rulers of the darkness of this world, against spiritual wickedness in high places"

(vv. 11–12). We must recognize the spirit of fear when it comes rushing in trying to sow doubt into our minds, and we must combat it by holding up the shield of faith, whereby we are able to quench all the fiery darts of the wicked (Eph. 6:16). As we trust God to be Jehovah Rapha, the Lord our Healer, He will move on our behalf.

God uses various avenues to bring healing. At times He will use the hand of a doctor or a surgeon. In other cases divine healings occur through the laying on of hands and the pure power of intercessory prayer. I am confident that miracles are still happening and that God responds to the faith of the His people (Matt. 9:29).

The Bible is clear on the subject of healing:

> Beloved, I wish above all things that thou mayest prosper and be in health, even as thy soul prospereth.
>
> —3 JOHN 2

> If thou wilt diligently hearken to the voice of the LORD thy God, and wilt do that which is right in his sight, and wilt give ear to his commandments, and keep all his statutes, I will put none of these diseases upon thee, which I have brought upon the Egyptians: for I am the LORD that healeth thee.
>
> —EXODUS 15:26

> For I will restore health unto thee, and I will heal thee of thy wounds, saith the LORD.
>
> —JEREMIAH 30:17

> But unto you that fear my name shall the Sun of righteousness arise with healing in his wings.
>
> —MALACHI 4:2

I will praise thee; for I am fearfully and wonderfully made: marvellous are thy works; and that my soul knoweth right well.

—Psalm 139:14

This is not a promise just for certain people or for Old Testament times. God has not changed, and healing is for you and me—*today.* Jesus Christ suffered horrible punishment and died on the cross so that we could be healed. The Bible says, "He was wounded for our transgressions, he was bruised for our iniquities: the chastisement of our peace was upon him; and with his stripes we are healed" (Isa. 53:5). Healing is the children's bread.

There are times in our faith fight when we will be tested and tried; this is when the Word of God has to come alive in our spirits. Speaking God's Word during times of trial builds your faith and encourages your spirit. The Word of God teaches us to walk by faith and not by sight. Hebrews 10:38 reminds us that "the just shall live by faith." (See also Habakkuk 2:4.)

"Death and life are in the power of the tongue: and they that love it shall eat the fruit thereof" (Prov. 18:21). We have been granted authority through the power of the blood of Jesus. Use the precious blood of Jesus as an ointment, applying it daily to the area affected by illness.

Do this by being specific as you pray for healing. Speak to the area where there is discomfort or pain and prophetically declare healing and wholeness to your body in the name of the Lord. Keep decreeing and declaring that by the stripes of Jesus Christ you are healed. Don't be afraid to be bold in prayer. When he was sick unto death, King Hezekiah prayed, "O Lord, remember now how I have walked before thee in truth and with a perfect heart, and have done that which is good in thy sight" (2 Kings 20:1–3). The prophet Isaiah responded with the word of the Lord, saying, "I have heard thy prayer; I have seen thy tears: behold, I will heal thee…and I will add unto thy days fifteen years" (vv. 5–6).

Believe that God wants to heal, and stand in faith on God's Word. The Lord will answer in His timing and in His way. We serve a God who still heals. Don't let the doctor's report convince you otherwise. Choose faith over fear.

Prayer for Physical Healing

Lord, Your Word says: "Is any among you afflicted? let him pray. Is any merry? let him sing psalms. Is any sick among you? let him call for the elders of the church; and let them pray over him, anointing him with oil in the name of the Lord: And the prayer of faith shall save the sick, and the Lord shall raise him up; and if he have committed sins, they shall be forgiven him" (James 5:13–15). Lord, You told us to confess our faults one to another, and pray one for another, that we may be healed, because "the effectual fervent prayer of a righteous man availeth much" (v. 16).

So, Lord, we apply and appropriate the precious shed blood of Jesus from the crown of the head to the soles of the feet. We pray for the systems of the body that have been affected by sickness and disease. We pray that the body will line up with the Word of God, which says that by Your stripes we are healed. We thank You that healing is available if we simply call upon You and ask.

By faith we speak to the respiratory system, the circulatory system, and the central nervous system, and command that they line up with Your will and function properly.

We agree in the Spirit concerning all issues of the heart and cardiovascular system, and all concerns of the digestive tract, esophagus, and stomach, including problems of the large and small intestines connected to the digestive system. We pray for the skeletal system, including the cartilage, tendons, and ligaments, and we lift up every gland and hormonal issue of the endocrine system—that they all function as You designed them to.

We pray for a regulated blood pressure in the name of the Lord. We ask, Lord, for healing from diabetes, cancer, and heart disease in the name of the Lord. We place the blood of Jesus in the brain, the cerebrum, cortex, cerebellum, and on every function that controls the body.

Father, we know that Your Word declares that You won't put more on us than we can bear. So today we thank You for healing every place where there is pain or discomfort now in Jesus's name. We declare that we shall be made whole according to the Word and the power of God. We say as Jesus did, "Rise and be healed in the name of Jesus of Nazareth." (See John 5:8.) We release miracles of healing this very moment in Jesus's name. We release faith to believe, despite the symptoms, that healing is imminent, and it is so in the matchless name of Jesus. Amen.

Chapter 12
BURNOUT FROM CAREGIVING

T HE DAN RYAN Expressway is an incredibly convenient highway in Chicago that leads into many areas of the city. Because it is such a major thoroughfare, it is often congested with traffic, especially between 7:00 a.m. and 9:00 a.m. If the Windy City has one of its infamous snow storms, the cars may literally be bumper to bumper as the snow is being plowed away.

When the weather is bad, often drivers will see large yellow emergency vehicles removing a car that may inhibit the traffic flow. These massive emergency vehicles are driven by a group called "Minute Men." These individuals, both male and female, are trained to drive through inclement weather conditions to help drivers whose cars are disabled on the side of the road.

Once I saw one of these massive emergency vehicles being towed by another truck. I remember thinking how strange it was to see an emergency vehicle in need of assistance. The more I thought about it, the more I saw it as a metaphor for caregivers. Those dedicated to helping others have a tendency to give and give to the point of burnout. Just as in the case of the towed emergency vehicle, there are times when a caregiver, no matter how loyal, diligent, and faithful, needs to stop and recover from years of service and help.

No matter what kind of vehicle you drive, it needs oil changes, tire rotations, and, yes, even an occasional car wash. Without the proper care, the car will not function properly and could break entirely. The same is true of people who are given to the service of others. They too need regular care in order to operate at their best. They need time to rest and refuel from the stress and strain that come with caring for others. If they don't take this time, they may burn out.

I am spending time on this subject because many people write to me saying they feel they are at the breaking point. They are caring for elderly parents, special-needs children, or a sick loved one, and they are exhausted because of the physical and emotional demands of their labor.

The time and patience required to care for others are incredible. Some caregivers seem to have a special gift; they care for others with such love and kindness. I am convinced that there are special blessings for these individuals who give so selflessly to make others comfortable. Hebrews 6:10 says, "For God is not unjust. He will not forget how hard you have worked for him and how you have shown your love to him by caring for other believers, as you still do" (NLT). I truly believe God will reward caregivers for their diligence and patience.

I know of a woman who personifies compassionate caregiving. Her daughter became ill when she was in her thirties, and she eventually lost the use of her arms and legs as paralysis overtook her body. This wonderful woman was determined to make her daughter comfortable and happy. Every morning she got up early to prepare breakfast for her husband and her daughter. Without a hint of a complaint, she bathed her daughter and brushed and combed her hair. She took responsibility for all of her daughter's needs, not out of a sense of duty but because she loved her. Over the years, as her daughter's health declined, I never once heard this woman complain.

Every time I visited her, I was always struck by her ability to keep an immaculate house even with so much on her plate. I was always so inspired by the love and peace I felt in her home. She always had some wonderful baked good to share along with an ice cold Pepsi. It was clear she had a gift for serving others.

When my mother was ill and facing her last days, my youngest sister, Tanya, served her tirelessly. Tanya had remarkable discernment concerning our mother. She knew what she needed even when our mother wasn't quite able to ask. Tanya was knowledgeable and efficient in assisting our mother in every way, as if she were a trained nurse. Although my other sisters and I offered to do anything we could to help, Tanya was so dedicated to caring for our mother, there was little for the rest of us to do.

Even during awkward and painful moments, Tanya had a way of making Mother laugh to the point that I believe she momentarily forgot about the pain. My sister worked so hard and never whispered a complaint. Our mother was a wonderful woman of God, and I know that Tanya will be rewarded in life for ministering to her in her time of need.

I thank God that He puts people around us to care so lovingly for the needs of others. Yet as I mentioned earlier, even the most giving person must have downtime in order to recover. Although it is desperately needed, taking time for themselves is one of the hardest things for caregivers to do. One reason is that they are so needed; there are few opportunities for them to take a few moments for themselves. Yet on the flip side, sometimes caregivers push themselves because they feel guilty for taking time to themselves or because they don't think they can trust someone else to offer care at the level they would. People are not like the Energizer Bunny. They won't keep going and going and going. They will burn out, and if that happens, who will be there to care for those precious loved ones?

Burnout is marked by physical and/or emotional

exhaustion. A person may become very tired and unmotivated or more susceptible to colds and viruses because stress compromises the immune system. Or the individual may become irritable and begin snapping at everyone. You know it's bad when you enter a room and the family dog runs to another part of the house. This is when it's obviously time for a break—a visit to a favorite restaurant, a massage, or even a couple days away from the person needing care.

This chapter is a kind of wake-up call for the "emergency vehicles." I believe I needed to include this chapter because the Holy Spirit wants caregivers to realize they are important to God too. Although the person they are caring for may have serious and significant needs, God did not place them in that person's life to run themselves into an early grave. He wants them to properly care for themselves so they will have the stamina to continue to pour His love out on others. If you are a caregiver or know one on the edge of burnout, please join me in this prayer:

Prayer for Caregivers

Lord, Your Word says that "it is of the Lord's mercies that we are not consumed, because [Your] compassions fail not. They are new every morning: great is thy faithfulness" (Lam. 3:22–23). So Lord, it is with joy that we come to You today, praying sincerely for those who care for others in various capacities. We ask You to bless them in a tremendous way. Let Your love and glory rest upon them.

We ask, Father, that You will deliver them from all irritation, agitation, and frustration. Lord, we thank You for even increasing their capacity to serve and to show Your love.

We come against the spirit of guilt that seeks to rob them of personal happiness. We pray for everyone experiencing stress and mental tiredness, and we ask that You would allow peace to flood their hearts and minds.

We loose the spirit of encouragement upon every faithful caregiver—from the loving family members to the nurses and medical assistants serving in hospitals and nursing homes. Bless them now, Lord, and let them know their labor is not in vain. Cover them in the precious blood of the Lord Jesus Christ and allow Your Holy Spirit to drive away all physical sickness and pain that would prevent them from serving.

We thank You for the individuals in the caregivers' care. We trust You, Lord, to bless them. Heal the sick and shut-in. Touch those with debilitating illnesses. Lord, Your Word declares that the power of life and death is in the tongue and they who love it shall eat the fruit thereof (Prov. 18:21). So we speak life upon every person in the care of this caregiver. We ask, Lord, that You work a miracle in them, body, mind, and soul.

Lord, we pray for physical strength for those who must exert themselves in order to assist others. Lord, give them wisdom and knowledge of proper procedure to avoid injury.

We pray also for a time of refreshing and restoration. Lord, we ask that You would open a door giving those who have been suffering from burnout a time to go on vacation and rest.

We are so grateful for Your grace and mercy. Lord, let the love of God be felt from the caregiver, and touch those in need of a miracle. God, You are sovereign and holy, and our trust is in You, our Maker and Creator. We count these things as done, in Jesus's name. Amen.

Chapter 13
PSYCHOLOGICAL ABUSE
AND MENTAL CRUELTY

I COUNT IT A tremendous honor to pray for those in need of a spiritual intervention. To sit next to someone and be trusted with a prayer need is a true blessing. We see many needs in our ministry, but one area of need that we see far too often is people wanting to break free of abusive relationships.

There was a time in our ministry when most of the people seeking prayer about abusive situations were facing physical abuse. I distinctly remember praying with a woman once who wore dark sunglasses during the entire church service to hide a black eye. Others came forward for prayer with makeup masking purple bruises and discolorations caused by punches and slaps.

Over time the prayer requests in this area have changed. Instead of physical abuse, we are seeing more people seeking prayer for psychological abuse and mental cruelty. In this kind of abuse a person is subjected to behavior that may result in psychological trauma, including anxiety, depression, and stress disorders.

There are three types of psychological abuse that I would like to highlight in this chapter: verbal aggression, dominant controlling behavior, and jealousy. Verbal aggression occurs when someone uses harmful and insulting words to upset or devalue another person. A person displays dominant controlling behavior when he or she purposefully prevents someone from having normal contact with family and friends, thus leaving the victim in a place of isolation. And the third area, jealousy, is marked by constant angry accusations that another party is maintaining inappropriate relationships.

These three types of emotional abuse can systematically diminish another individual. They can crush a person's spirit, whether the abuse is intentional or subconscious. Sadly, the scars of this kind of abuse are not always easy to see. Psychological abuse destroys a person's self-worth and self-esteem. Because we are connected mind, body, and spirit, emotional abuse can also manifest in physical ways, such as illness or mental breakdown.

When talking with victims of emotional abuse, I seek to help them understand why this kind of treatment occurs. Many times those who are emotionally abusive will give affection intermittently and mix kindness with their abusive behavior. Some victims will endure the abuse just for those moments of love and affection, thinking it is better to endure the hostility than to be alone.

For those on the outside looking in on the abusive relationship, it is often hard to understand why an abuse victim doesn't leave. There is such a thing as "capture-bonding." It is a psychological phenomenon in which a victim forms a bond with his or her captor. This strong emotional tie can develop even in cases when the victim is being harassed, threatened, and intimidated. The longer the victims are held captive, the more empathy they begin to feel toward the captors, even to the point of defending them.

Capture-bonding and the longing for love explain why the victim stays, but let's take a minute to examine what motivates the abuser. Many abusers are narcissistic, meaning their personalities are characterized by egotism, vain conceit, and selfishness. Narcissists have an inordinate fascination with themselves, and their preoccupation with their own aspirations, needs, and desires is all-consuming. Some narcissists are charismatic and charming, but their grandiosity and love for themselves lead them to become cold, manipulative, and angry when they don't get what they want.

As you might imagine, abusers often use mind games. They deliberately behave in certain ways for psychological effect. Their behavior may be erratic and unpredictable to make the victim feel frustrated and unstable. They may be cold one minute and hot the next, "on" one minute and "off" the next, to cause confusion. They may send mixed signals and toy with emotions—all in an attempt to control or to elicit a particular reaction from the victim.

After enduring these minds games for so long, many times the victims will give the abusers the response they want. That is often when the abuser will point a finger back at the victim, calling his or her reaction "crazy."

Breaking free of abusive situations is not easy. Very often in these cases of abuse and control an ungodly soul tie has been formed. A soul tie develops between people who are extremely close. The Bible says "the soul of Jonathan was knit with the soul of David, and Jonathan loved him as his own soul" (1 Sam. 18:1). And we read in Genesis 2:24, "Therefore a man shall leave his father and his mother and shall become united and cleave to his wife, and they shall become one flesh" (AMP).

God wants us to have relationships that honor Him, but unhealthy relationships can lead to unhealthy soul ties. Engaging in sex outside of marriage or idolizing a person can produce an unhealthy soul tie that brings bondage to the soul. If a person is ever to experience lasting freedom from unhealthy situations, the ties must be broken in the name of Jesus.

In order to break soul ties, one must repent of any sin committed with that person and receive God's forgiveness. Then she must renounce any vows or covenants made with the individual and loose herself from any ungodly soul ties she may have formed with that individual. She will also need to forgive the person for any wrongs committed against her.

Breaking the unhealthy soul tie will help remove the blinders so the person can see the truth about the relationship. Then he or she can invite the Holy Spirit to bring freedom and wholeness.

Prayer for Victims of Psychological Abuse

Father God, You are our God. We thank You for revelation knowledge and for the truth. Lord, we ask You today to extend Your hand of mercy to every victim of psychological abuse. We pray now in the name of Jesus that You would send angels with swords of fire dipped in the purifying blood of Jesus to sever every demonic stronghold of control, domination, and intermittent affection. We address all traumas stemming from mind games that were used to destabilize the mind and devastate the soul.

We break the power of calculated psychological manipulation designed to confuse and challenge the intellect. We destroy the power of intimidation, domination, and manipulation now, in the name of Jesus. We pray that You will expose every entryway that the enemy has used to create ungodly soul ties. Father, we sever every spirit of capture-bonding, the spirit that feels false empathy and sympathy toward one's abuser.

We break every unhealthy and ungodly soul tie that
has formed through the spirit of seduction, lust, and sexual
promiscuity, in the name of Jesus. We break the power
of rejection, self-rejection, and low self-esteem that has
been strengthened by an unhealthy soul tie. We pray for
freedom in the mind and in the thought patterns, in Jesus's
name.

Father, we decree and declare freedom from the damage
of every spoken word, curse, or abusive term that has
caused the victim to feel worthless and useless. We pray
for deliverance and deep healing for those who have been
affected physically by the abuse. We pray for restoration of
damaged nerves, areas affected by stress, and an end to all
fear and anxiety.

This is a prayer of intervention to prevent more damage,
and we say the abuse will cease today. Lord, Your Word
declares that we have been given authority and dominion
over every demonic assignment, in Jesus's name. We loose
the power of Jesus Christ to bind up the brokenhearted
and to let the oppressed go free. We bind every spirit that
makes one feel powerless, for Your Word says You give us
the victory and cause us to triumph through Jesus Christ
our Lord (2 Cor. 2:14). We declare victory this day. In
Jesus's precious name we pray, amen.

Chapter 14
OTHER ABUSIVE RELATIONSHIPS

IN THE PREVIOUS chapter we prayed for victims of psychological abuse and mental cruelty. In this chapter I want to discuss ways to pray for those caught in other kinds of abusive relationships.

In order to pray effectively for a person suffering in an abusive relationship, it is needful to look at how the abuse begins. Abuse is a gradual process. Typically a relationship begins with showers of love and affection—sweet words, cards, and loving letters. This can be exhilarating, especially if the person has not had much attention from the opposite sex. Being noticed makes a person feel special.

As the two spend more time together, the friendship deepens and a bond develops. Unbeknownst to the victim, the abusive person is soaking up details about the victim's life. With this information the abuser will seek to control the other person, knowing the victim's strengths and weaknesses, hopes and fears, successes and failures.

Over time the proverbial red flags go up, but the victims often ignore them because of their happiness over being in the relationship. They sincerely believe they have fallen in love, and they choose to become blind to controlling behavior and abusive traits. If they do notice the behavior, or if friends or family members point it out to them, they may excuse it. Their judgment is clouded, and they cannot clearly see what is happening.

It is frustrating for those around the individual in the abusive situation. You see your loved one walking into a trap, and when you try to bring it to their attention, they dismiss you. It is important that you do not let offense or a spirit of rejection take root in your heart. They do this because they fear losing the relationship or because they fear confronting the abusive individual.

As time goes by, the possessive traits of the controlling person become more obvious. The controlling person may become determined to keep tabs on the victim, constantly asking questions such as: "Where are you going? Who with? What time will you return?" Or, "Why haven't you called?"

Another trait of a controlling person is that he or she may constantly need to know the victim's state of mind or intentions. You may also notice a sense of confusion in the victim when made to think he or she is disappointing the controlling person. A pattern of anxiety and fear may manifest because the victim feels a need to constantly please the other person.

This controlling pattern may lead to either mental or physical abuse. This happens both inside and outside the church. Domestic violence breaks the spirit and causes a person to live in constant fear. It is a crime to terrorize, harass, or force a person to engage in an activity, but abuse victims rarely know how to break free.

It is critical that we pray effectively for those in this situation. First, we must arrest the spirit of low self-worth and low self-esteem that would make someone willing to endure mental cruelty, abusive words, or physical violence.

If a person has had a lifetime of rejection, breaking free of an abusive relationship is even harder, because a rejected person has a tendency to cling to anyone who accepts him or her. A controlling person is aware of this weakness and exploits it. Often the abuser will punish through withdrawal or by ignoring the person and giving the silent treatment (also called "stonewalling," which is when someone refuses to engage in conversation during a discussion or disagreement). In this way they keep the victim under their influence. If we understand the abuser's behavior, we will be able to pray more effectively.

If there has been a sexual relationship, the soul tie formed between the individuals must be severed as we discussed in the previous chapter. During prayer it is vital to break the strong bond that has developed through sexual contact, especially if the controlling person has used the withdrawal of affection as a form of punishment.

In prayer it is also necessary to ask the Lord to deliver the soul (mind, will, and emotions) from the power of this controlling and abusive spirit. In prayer we ask God to restore the fragmented pieces of the soul to the victim. It is also necessary to bind mind control and mind-commandeering spirits that harass and torment.

Often during prayer the victim may feel depressed and devastated and have a hopeless outlook, thinking that no one will be able to fill the void left by the abusive person. This is a lie from the enemy and must be confronted along with the other demonic strongholds at work in these kinds of situations.

If you have a loved one who is in an abusive relationship and needs a spiritual intervention, I encourage you to pray the following prayer with me. As I said in chapter 1, there is power in agreement. One can put a thousand demons to flight, but two can put ten thousand to flight. So let's pray.

PRAYER FOR INDIVIDUALS IN ABUSIVE RELATIONSHIPS

Father, in Jesus's name, we intercede for those caught in abusive relationships. We release the healing balm of Gilead to heal the soul that is fragmented and torn by abusive behavior. We ask You, Lord, to release Your angels to do battle on behalf of the victim. Thank You, Lord, for breaking the power of fear and torment and all harassing spirits.

We break every spirit that makes it seem OK to tolerate being punched or hit repeatedly. Father, we ask that You give Your child courage to remove himself/herself from harm's way. Lord, restore [name the individual]'s soul to a place of wholeness and freedom. In the name of Jesus we rebuke the assignment of fear that would lead a person to return to the abusive partner under the false hope that the person will change. We release the dunamis, or "mighty," power of God to destroy, cut, and sever every stronghold of low self-esteem, low self-worth, and low value. Every spirit that tolerates control, anger, contempt, and criticism, we bind now.

Father, give them the strength to overcome the systematic cycle of devaluation of their thoughts and opinions. Father, give them a voice and the courage to expose the abusive behavior and to request help and deliverance. We apply and appropriate the blood of Jesus to every area of the heart that has been devastated by abuse, and we release a spirit of hope. We pray for wisdom to allow God to order their steps to a place of refuge and safety.

Lord, You came to bind up the wounds, heal the brokenhearted, and let the oppressed go free. I thank You, Lord, for absolute freedom and for peace that passes all understanding. In the name of Your Son, Jesus, we pray. Amen.

Spiritual Intervention for Spiritual Breakthrough

Chapter 15
SEXUAL BONDAGE

ONE DAY THE Lord spoke to me and said that one of the greatest problems the people of God are encountering is that the door to the imagination has remained open in the mind. God spent a lot of time in His Word warning us about the things we allow ourselves to see. That's because our eye gates open the windows to our souls. We connect directly with the things we observe with our eyes.

The Bible tells us, "The light of the body is the eye: if therefore thine eye be single, thy whole body shall be full of light. But if thine eye be evil, thy whole body shall be full of darkness. If therefore the light that is in thee be darkness, how great is that darkness!" (Matt. 6:22–23).

Every day we decide what we will entertain. There are those who have a made-up mind to live holy and acceptable unto the Lord. They make a concerted effort to consistently keep the commandments and statues of the Lord. But there are others who live to satisfy their flesh, seeking their own pleasure. They may be Christians, but they are following a soulish path and are fulfilling the desires of the flesh rather than the will of God.

The soul is comprised of the mind, the will, and the emotions. The Bible tells us, "They that are after the flesh do mind the things of the flesh; but they that are after the Spirit the things of the Spirit. For to be carnally minded is death; but to be spiritually minded is life and peace" (Rom. 8:5–6). Notice that the verse says those who are after the flesh "do mind the things of the flesh." What we dwell on will lead us either to death or to life and peace.

Our greatest battle is in the mind! The mind is quite unique because it stores information and recalls it like a computer. This is one reason it is so important to screen the things you see and hear. Entertaining the soulish realm with constant lustful images opens the door to demonic activity and fleshly battles.

There are many carnally minded Christians. To be carnal means to be led by the appetites of the unsanctified, materialistic flesh. There are many Christians whose flesh is stronger than their spirit.

These individuals usually walk in compromise as well. Compromise is a silent endorsement of the world's ways and a consent to walk according to its standards. After giving in to compromise for so long, eventually love for the world will dominate the spirit and outweigh love for the Father.

Second Corinthians 10:4–5 tells us, "(For the weapons of our warfare are not carnal, but mighty through God to the pulling down of strong holds;) casting down imaginations, and every high thing that exalteth itself against the knowledge of God, and bringing into captivity every thought to the obedience of Christ." The Lord wants us to rise up and take authority over the flesh! So let's take a closer look at what 2 Corinthians 10:5 is telling us about disciplining our thoughts and winning the battle for the mind.

Casting down imaginations. To *cast down imaginations* means to violently throw down formed pictures in the mind and things not immediately present to the senses—all the vain images that the world uses to get our attention.

And every high thing that exalts itself against the knowledge of God. We must *cast down* our own reasoning. God is omniscient, which means He's all-knowing, and when we to try to figure out things to come, we are interfering with the process of trusting the Lord for His perfect will to be done in our lives.

Bringing into captivity every thought. To *bring into captivity every thought* is to take captive all carnal reasoning and opinions.

To the obedience of Christ. To be under *the obedience of Christ* is to totally submit to the Word of God and the commandments of Christ.

We can pull down every stronghold by applying the powerful shed blood of Jesus to our minds and thoughts. We can bind the work of the enemy in our thought life (Matt. 18:18), and we can overcome the works of the flesh by bringing the flesh into subjection to the Spirit. Colossians 3:5 exhorts us, "Mortify therefore your members which are upon the earth." That means we are to crucify the flesh.

Why must we crucify our flesh? The Bible is clear: "For if ye live after the flesh, ye shall die: but if ye through the Spirit do mortify the deeds of the body, ye shall live" (Rom. 8:13). The apostle Paul also wrote, "I beseech you therefore, brethren, by the mercies of God, that ye present your bodies a living sacrifice, holy, acceptable unto God, which is your reasonable service. And be not conformed to this world: but be ye transformed by the renewing of your mind, that ye may prove what is that good, and acceptable, and perfect, will of God" (Rom. 12:1–2).

Dying to self is not easy, and it may require times of fasting and prayer. Fasting humbles the soul and brings the flesh into subjection to the spirit. When we fast, we deny the flesh and feed the spirit. Self-denial strengthens the Spirit of Christ within us, deepens our walk with the Lord, and empowers our prayer life.

Whatever you feed the most will grow. If you feed the

spirit with prayer and Bible study, it will flourish. But if you spend more time feeding the flesh and the carnal sin nature, the flesh will dominate.

Many people have found themselves in sexual bondage because they feed their flesh with pornographic images. The spirit of lust uses pornography to create an intense sexual desire or appetite. Then the spirit of lasciviousness creates an insatiable desire to satisfy those lewd and lustful desires. This is how viewing porn becomes addictive. After seeing a little, people are driven to see more until they feel unable to stop.

Sexual bondage can be broken in the name of Jesus. In this chapter I have included a prayer for those making intercession on another's behalf, as well as a prayer for the individual in crisis. We can pray for others and God will answer, but in order to remain free, the individual must abandon the activity that opened the door to the enemy. So in addition to receiving prayer for deliverance from sexual bondage, those in crisis should pray the prayer below. It will guide them in closing the legal entry they have given to demonic spirits and declaring themselves a new creature in Christ.

PRAYERS TO BREAK SEXUAL BONDAGE

Father, Your Word declares in Romans 12:1 that we are to present our bodies as a living sacrifice holy and acceptable unto You, for this is our reasonable service. Lord, help us by transforming and renewing our minds. Father, we know if we walk in the flesh we cannot please You. As an act of our will we renounce every spirit of pornography, lust, and lasciviousness. We break the bondage in the mind that is connected to ungodly images. Father, we

*apply and appropriate the cleansing blood of Jesus to satu-
rate our minds and drive out every unclean spirit.*

*We pray now for every person who gave place to the
enemy as a child by reading materials that were inappropriate. We loose them from every hidden desire that is displeasing to You, Lord. We thank You, Lord, for the light
of Your Word that shines on every dark place. Lord, Your
Word says to guard the heart, for out of it proceeds the
issues of life. We thank You that we are redeemed this day
by the blood of Jesus, and we declare freedom. In Jesus's
name, amen!*

For the individual in crisis:

*Lord God, I come to You in the name of Jesus. You are
my strong deliverer. You know all the things that defile,
torment, and harass Your children. Your Word says in
Matthew 18:18 that whatsoever we shall bind on earth
shall be bound in heaven: and whatsoever we shall loose
on earth shall be loosed in heaven. I thoroughly repent of
and denounce all sins of the flesh. I forgive every person
who has violated me in any way. I denounce the spirits
that gained access to me through sexual immorality or vio-
lation. I break the assignments over my family line back
a thousand generations. I break every curse, and I accept
the provision of Christ Jesus, for Christ has redeemed me
from the curse of the law (Gal. 3:13).*

*I rebuke all legal rights I gave any of these spirits that
allowed them access to my life. I apply the blood of Jesus
Christ and loose upon myself the spirit of deliverance. I
ask, Lord, that You send warring angels to join the angels
of the Lord that are encamped around me right now. I*

hate and curse all that is wicked and abominable to You, in the name of Jesus Christ.

I agree in the spirit with the person(s) who is standing with me in prayer that these are demonic influences and infestations, and that they must leave me now. I bind all evil spirits that commonly operate alongside spirits of homosexuality and perversion. I bind masturbation and a self-abusing spirit. I bind self-gratification; self-love; pride; imaginary sexual activity; impotency; fantasy; arrogance; vanity; inferiority; doubt about masculinity or femininity; spirits that drive repeated sexual affairs; tormenting spirits; insatiable desire; spirits of ravishment, enchantment, infatuation, and sensuality; roving and wandering eyes; whoremongering; adultery; uncleanness; effeminate behavior among men; fornication; sexual deviance; dishonor; scorn; and reproach. I also bind rejection and all spirits connected to it.

I come against all demonic authorities that have controlled and motivated my relationship with certain friends. I bind every spirit that entered in through incest, molestation, fondling, and perversion, in the name of Jesus.

I break every demonic spirit that attacks the mind with ungodly thoughts. I remove myself by the blood of Jesus Christ from all perverse, ungodly activity, and I break every soul tie and all wrong affections. Lord, I thank You for total freedom in Your name. Satan, I submit myself to God totally, and resist you. You must flee in Jesus's name. Go! Go! Go!

Father, I ask that You reveal all sexual offenses that I did not renounce. I am a new creature in Christ; old things have passed away, and I now have become new in You. Thank You, Jesus, for delivering and setting me free. Amen!

Chapter 16
POVERTY

POVERTY IS A state or condition of having little or no money. Poverty has a way of dominating the human spirit; it can rob individuals of their joy and bring depression. Poverty is a cyclical, demonic assignment that causes lack and debt. When it is present, the debt becomes insurmountable and makes an individual feel as if he is literally drowning. The spirit of poverty comes to steal every blessing that comes into a person's life and choke the hope of advancement. Those oppressed by poverty often feel like they're always taking two steps forward and three steps back.

I know from experience how this spirit operates. For a season it seemed that no matter how much my family tried, we just could not get ahead. Something would always happen that caused a financial setback.

When I was a senior in high school, my parents, three sisters, and I were living in a rented home in a nice area on the South Side of Chicago. We were renting the house from an African couple who was going through a horrible divorce. The property became part of the divorce settlement, and we were told to vacate the home in thirty days. Imagine trying to find a place for a family of six in such a short period of time. Needless to say, we were in a terrible dilemma.

We began to desperately look for another place to live. We tried petitioning the courts to give us more time, but nothing helped. My sister Cheryl and I were both working in the downtown area at the time. Cheryl worked at the Secretary of State's office, and after school I worked at the American Library Association as a clerical typist. Our father worked as a custodial engineer, and our mom was an evangelist. We were all trying to make ends meet.

We didn't realize it, but we were fighting a spirit of poverty. If it wasn't the car transmission that was broken, it was the refrigerator. One bad thing would happen after another. We would all put our money together and work as a family to get ahead, yet there was always something waiting to rob our increase.

I remember the day the sheriff came to evict us from our home. I took the bus to the stop closest to our house. As I walked down the street toward our home, I saw large pieces of our furniture in the backyard. I kept walking and saw the rest of our belongings in the front yard. I was stunned and devastated to see everything we owned sitting outside.

I felt defeated in that moment, but just when I would have hit rock bottom, I saw my older sister Denise in front of the house. She had been home ill that day, and as I walked around the corner I found her sitting on our stereo cabinet, swinging her legs, and, to my shock and dismay, yelling, "Yard sale!" while laughing and waving to people who were slowing down in front of the house. Denise has always been known for her hilarious sense of humor, and she has always had remarkable strength and resilience during times of crisis.

My mother, a mighty woman of God and a prayer warrior, was sitting on the front steps with a telephone in hand. The sheriff was kind enough to allow her to keep the phone cord plugged up inside the home so that we could call someone to help us move our furniture. All of this was happening just days before I was to graduate from high school. Needless to say, this was an incredibly challenging time for us.

My father rented a U-Haul truck, and we were able to park it for several days with our belongings inside while we continued to search for a home. When one of our church mothers heard of our terrible dilemma, she offered to let us stay in her one-bedroom apartment located in a building designated for senior citizens. We were so grateful to have a place to stay for the night. Our entire family—all six of us—crammed into the church mother's apartment, and she prepared food and cared for us without complaint.

On the day of my graduation, no one in my class knew that my family had been evicted only days before. I was asked to sing for our graduation ceremony, which was held on a Sunday morning at a venue downtown. I was chosen to sing after being named Most Talented Senior, and I sang "I Know Who Holds Tomorrow." The song says I don't worry about the future because I know the One who knows what lies ahead.

Many church people were attending the graduation. During the song my mother was praising the Lord and shouting hallelujah despite the fact that everything we owned was still in the U-Haul truck. After my family started worshipping, it started a chain reaction of rejoicing at the graduation ceremony. We didn't know where we would go, but through hope, hard work, and the power of prayer, we broke through a strong spirit of poverty that was plaguing us.

We were determined to pray our way out of that situation. During our stay with the church mother, our family bonded in a way that we never had before. Our love for one another grew stronger as we prayed together in those small quarters. We worked together as a family. For a time we could not buy very much, but we kept putting our finances together until we were able to move into our own home in the southern suburbs.

Until There's Nothing Left

The spirit of poverty works in a variety of ways, but its goal is to rob a person of abundance and deplete all income sources until there is nothing left. It may affect a person's thinking so they develop habits that create a cycle of defeat. They may dig themselves deep in debt buying things they can't afford just to impress the Joneses of this world. Or they may adopt an attitude of defeat by thinking they can never get ahead. In some cases a poverty spirit has been present in a family for decades.

In order to break the spirit of poverty, we must take some very practical steps. We must live within our means and pay our bills on time. We must make financial decisions based on what we can afford within our budget and not on what impresses people. And we must be faithful in our giving in obedience to the Word of God. Scripture tells us:

> Give, and it shall be given unto you; good measure, pressed down, and shaken together, and running over, shall men give into your bosom. For with the same measure that ye mete withal it shall be measured to you again.
> —Luke 6:38

> He which soweth sparingly shall reap also sparingly; and he which soweth bountifully shall reap also bountifully. Every man according as he purposeth in his heart, so let him give; not grudgingly, or of necessity: for God loveth a cheerful giver.
> —2 Corinthians 9:6–7

> Will a man rob God? Yet ye have robbed me. But ye say, Wherein have we robbed thee? In tithes and offerings.... Bring ye all the tithes into the storehouse, that there may be meat in mine house, and prove me now herewith, saith the Lord of hosts, if I will not open you the windows

of heaven, and pour you out a blessing, that there shall not be room enough to receive it. And I will rebuke the devourer for your sakes, and he shall not destroy the fruits of your ground; neither shall your vine cast her fruit before the time in the field, saith the LORD of hosts.

—MALACHI 3:8, 10–11

Honour the LORD with thy substance, and with the first-fruits of all thine increase.

—PROVERBS 3:9

Disobedience in the area of giving creates an open door to the spirit of poverty. It gives the adversary a legal right to attack a child of God. We broke through the strong spirit of poverty that was plaguing us by consistently tithing and faithfully giving in offerings.

While the Bible instructs us to give bountifully, we are not to become either proud or ashamed of the amount we give. God weighs the intentions and motives of our hearts when we give. What He wants is our obedience.

Even if a family has lived in poverty for generations, they do not have to remain under a generational curse. The Word of God gives us authority over the spirit of poverty, and we can break its hold even on a family line. Those who are in Christ are Abraham's seed and heirs to the covenant of blessing God made with him. We serve a God who is more than able to supply our every need. We can initiate generational blessings by taking dominion over the spirit of poverty and walking in obedience to the Word of God.

PRAYER FOR BREAKING A SPIRIT OF POVERTY

Eternal Father, we come to You thanking You for an opportunity to surrender our financial dealings to You. We thank You for this time of introspection. We confess that there have been times when we have not been obedient in the area of giving. We renounce every wrong spirit that has affected our patterns of giving in the past. We repent for the times when we did not give in tithes and offerings. We confess our faults and ask forgiveness. We forgive every person of any offense concerning debt of every kind.

We also ask Your forgiveness for:

- *Every sin of commission and omission*
- *Being dishonest in paying bills and avoiding debt collectors*
- *Thinking that debtors do not need or deserve to be paid because they are wealthy*
- *Not giving to the poor*
- *Not being consistent and faithful in giving*

Father, we ask that You break every generational curse and hindrance the enemy has placed on our finances, in Jesus's name. We bind the spirits of poverty, covetousness, stealing, and lying; the fear of poverty, fear of the future, and fear of change; ungratefulness; unholiness; unforgiveness; manipulation; a poverty mentality; violence; disrespect for others; inherited curses; treachery; defeatism; melancholy; dishonesty; misappropriation of funds; wrong decisions; and theft.

Father, we break the power of the carnivorous spirit at the root of gambling, playing the lottery, and pursuing false chances of quick wealth. We come against the vagabond spirit, discontentment, indolence, laziness, lethargy, slothfulness, passivity, lack, uncleanness, hopelessness, and disdain. Lord, we know that these are all things the enemy uses to keep us in financial lack.

Now, Lord, we thank You for accepting our repentance. Today we break every spirit of poverty. We bind the stronghold of pride that seeks to impress others with material things that we cannot afford. We bind the spirit of deception that causes a person to live above his means to impress others. We come against the fear that the cycle will not be broken.

We destroy every stronghold operating through generational curses or sin doors opened willingly or unwillingly. We break the cycle of financial debt and bondage. We break the spirit of lack, want, and entitlement. We declare that our finances are blessed.

Lord, Your Word declares, "But thou shalt remember the Lord thy God: for it is he that giveth thee power to get wealth, that he may establish his covenant which he sware unto thy fathers, as it is this day" (Deut. 8:18).

Father, we loose every investment, every inheritance, and all that God has designed for us to have. We loose upon ourselves the wealth of the unjust that is laid up for the righteous.

We thank You for the Holy Ghost who gives us power over the enemy. We thank You that all of our needs are supplied and met in Jesus's name. Thank You, Lord, for setting us free!

We declare this day freedom and liberation from the spirit of poverty. Your Word declares that the power of life and death is in our tongue. We declare and decree that the blessings of Abraham, Isaac, and Jacob be released over our lives and our families according to the Word of God. Thank You, Lord, for a new beginning of debt-free living.

Lord, we declare that You shall command the blessing upon us in our storehouses, and in all that we set our hand unto; and You shall bless us in the land which You, the Lord our God, giveth us (Deut. 28:8). These things we pray in the matchless name of Jesus. Amen.

Declaration to Become a Holy Millionaire

Lord God, in the mighty name of Jesus, You said in Deuteronomy 8:18 that You give me power to receive wealth that You may establish Your covenant with me. Lord Jesus, I am a joint heir with You, and I have an inheritance among them that are sanctified. You came that I might have life and that more abundantly. You told me to seek first the kingdom of God, and all of its righteousness; and all of these other things shall be added unto me (Matt. 6:33). I declare that I will seek You above any material need or want that I may have. You are able to do exceeding abundantly above all that I could ask or think.

You said the gold and silver in the heart of the earth belong to You. You said the earth is Yours and the fullness thereof, the world and they that dwell therein. Lord God, You change not. I will not rob You in tithes and offerings. You told me to prove You. Lord, You are opening Your heavenly windows, and I receive Your overflowing blessings.

I thank You that You are rebuking the devourer for my sake. I thank You that the fruit of our vines will be blessed and timely. I thank You that I am a delightsome land. My *hands are blessed. My feet are blessed. You have blessed my going out and my coming in. I am blessed!*

Lord, I thank You that my words have become Your words and I speak them often. I thank You that I am Your jewel and You have given me great discernment. I stand not in self-righteousness but in the righteousness of God. The power of life and death is in my tongue—You placed it there, Lord Jesus.

Because You said that I can have what I say (Mark 11:23), I declare that I have an eye to see and receive the wealth that is being shaken out of the hand of the wicked, to upbuild and declare the kingdom of our God. I declare that:

I am rich in grace.

I am rich in mercy.

I am rich in love.

I am holy.

I am redeemed by the blood of the Lamb.

I am a joint heir with Christ.

I am a holy millionaire!

Chapter 17
SPIRITUAL DRYNESS

THE HEART OF a person who has lost his place of intimacy with God or who is backslidden is similar to the dry, parched conditions of a desert. In the desert few forms of life can exist because of the lack of water. Without a continual water supply, it is difficult for plants, animals, and people to survive. In the same way, a person whose heart has become spiritually dry and barren has a hard time bearing godly fruit. They often display a coldness. Even in times of prayer there is a lack of contrition and brokenness.

The Bible says the heart is desperately wicked. Who can know the heart but God? When David sinned against God by committing adultery with Bathsheba, the prophet Nathan had to help him see the error of his ways (2 Sam. 12). Yet when he realized what he had done, he cried out to the Lord in prayer:

> Have mercy upon me, O God, according to thy lovingkindness: according unto the multitude of thy tender mercies blot out my transgressions.
> Wash me thoroughly from mine iniquity, and cleanse me from my sin.
> For I acknowledge my transgressions: and my sin is ever before me.
> Against thee, thee only, have I sinned, and done this evil in thy sight: that thou mightest be justified when thou speakest, and be clear when thou judgest.
> Behold, I was shapen in iniquity; and in sin did my mother conceive me.
> Behold, thou desirest truth in the inward parts: and in the hidden part thou shalt make me to know wisdom.

Purge me with hyssop, and I shall be clean: wash me, and I
shall be whiter than snow.

Make me to hear joy and gladness; that the bones which
thou hast broken may rejoice.

Hide thy face from my sins, and blot out all mine iniquities.

Create in me a clean heart, O God; and renew a right spirit
within me.

Cast me not away from thy presence; and take not thy holy
spirit from me.

Restore unto me the joy of thy salvation; and uphold me
with thy free spirit.

Then will I teach transgressors thy ways; and sinners shall
be converted unto thee.

Deliver me from bloodguiltiness, O God, thou God of my salvation: and my tongue shall sing aloud of thy righteousness.

O Lord, open thou my lips; and my mouth shall shew forth
thy praise.

For thou desirest not sacrifice; else would I give it: thou
delightest not in burnt offering.

The sacrifices of God are a broken spirit: a broken and a
contrite heart, O God, thou wilt not despise.

Do good in thy good pleasure unto Zion: build thou the
walls of Jerusalem.

Then shalt thou be pleased with the sacrifices of righteousness, with burnt offering and whole burnt offering: then
shall they offer bullocks upon thine altar.

—Psalm 51

David knew his sin would separate him from God, so he
was willing to confess his fault, knowing that a broken and
contrite heart God would not despise. The Lord was faithful
to forgive him and restore the fellowship with God that he
once enjoyed.

It is sin that causes us to become spiritually dry. One of

the most common definitions of sin is missing the mark or failing to live up to an expected standard. Another definition of sin is found in 1 John 3:4: "Sin is the transgression of the law." That means sin is anything that is contrary to what the Word of God commands. Put more simply, "All unrighteousness is sin," as 1 John 5:17 declares.

We may have experienced disappointment or loss that caused us to doubt God's faithfulness. We may have become complacent in praying and studying God's Word, causing our faith in God's promises to become weak. Small, subtle things like these can cause us to drift away from the Lord.

Christ Jesus represents a well of living water. When a person is in a spiritually dry or lukewarm state, there is a clear absence of the joy, happiness, and peace that Jesus Christ gives.

There is a process called *gradualism* that leads to spiritual disconnection. A person becomes cold, distant, and disinterested in the things of God *over time*. It starts with listening to the spirit of the world and allowing it to be a stronger influence than God. A person pursues his own desires instead of spending time in God's presence. Then it becomes hard to recapture that place of intimacy.

As a pastor I've come to recognize some clear signs that a person is in a critical spiritual place:

Offense. A person who is not walking closely with the Lord will often have an unspoken, unprovoked disdain for the church, the people of God, and especially people who are joyful and living an abundant life. Those who are spiritually disconnected often have strong critical spirits that cause them to find fault in people they once respected. It is a spirit of offense that creates breaches among individuals who genuinely love one another. If not checked, the spirit of offense will destroy friendships and relationships.

Change in conversation. The Bible says that out of the abundance of the heart the mouth speaketh (Matt. 12:34; Luke 6:45). A second sign I've noticed among people who are drifting from their first love is that their conversation changes. I have observed that a backsliding person has a tendency to completely avoid conversations about the Lord. Typically their conversation is marked by carnality.

Anger. A third sign of spiritual disconnection is that the person may have angry outbursts. Anger is a clear indicator that someone is holding on to an offense. Unforgiveness separates us from the presence of God. The Bible tells us, "But if ye forgive not men their trespasses, neither will your Father forgive your trespasses" (Matt. 6:15). And, "When ye stand praying, forgive, if ye have ought against any: that your Father also which is in heaven may forgive you your trespasses" (Mark 11:25).

Unforgiveness will lead to a spiritually dry place. When people are accustomed to feeling God's love and presence, they often feel lost when they're unable to sense Him. They don't realize that they may be feeling disconnected from God's presence because they are refusing to forgive. Forgiveness is an act of the will. Once forgiveness and restoration of mind, body, and spirit have occurred, love, joy, and gratitude for all of the things He has done will come flooding in.

It's painful to see a person who is lost in a world of disappointments, bitterness, and hostility, and cut off from the presence of God. This is a dangerous place. Don't let the cares of life or men with human frailties keep you from the presence of God. Do as David did and return to the Lord.

Habakkuk prayed, "O Lord, revive thy work in the midst of the years, in the midst of the years make known; in wrath remember mercy" (Hab. 3:2). If you are in a spiritually dry place, God remembers mercy and He hears your prayer. You can be restored today.

Prayer for Spiritual Dryness

Father, Your Word teaches that the heart is desperately wicked. Who can know the heart but God? So today we ask You to wash our hearts, Lord, to search us and try us and see if there be any wicked way in us. Create in us a clean heart and renew a right spirit within us. Holy Spirit, we ask that You would take out the stony, cold heart and give a heart of flesh.

We ask, Lord, that You will give clarity where there is disillusionment, hope where there is hopelessness, and love for the person who feels spiritually lost. We ask, Lord, that You will deliver [name the individual] from this dry, barren place and bring restoration in the realm of the spirit in Jesus's name. Breathe into Your people, O Lord, the breath of life.

We ask You, Lord, to lift every burden and care that has caused spiritual drought. Lord, release now Your Holy Spirit and allow the water of Your Word to spring up and bring refreshing. We ask for restoration, revival, and renewal of the spirit. Lord, let the glory of Your presence restore joy to the spirit. We release happiness and laughter that doeth good like a medicine to the soul. Father, place clapping in the hands, give beauty for ashes and the oil of joy for the spirit of heaviness. Lift up the bowed-down head and release an anointing that destroys every yoke. We honor You, Lord, for Your omnipotent power that is able to bring true liberation in Jesus's name. Amen.

Chapter 18
VIOLENCE IN OUR CITIES

Not long ago I had an opportunity to travel to Rome, Italy, and while I was there I visited the ancient Colosseum. It was an awesome architectural structure, and it was quite thrilling to see a place that, as the site of the gladiator battles, holds such an important place in world history.

During my incredible stay in Rome I was introduced to many people. Many times I was asked where I was from. When I told them I was born and raised in Chicago, located in the United States of America, to my surprise and dismay most would respond with a comment about one of Chicago's more famous residents. "Al Capone!" one gentleman said with enthusiasm. "Caponey!" as though he knew him personally.

I must be honest; I was disappointed that the city I love was primarily being associated with a notorious American gangster. Having been born and raised there, I know there are splendid areas of Chicago that are recognized worldwide for their elegance. The Magnificent Mile, sometimes referred to as The Mag Mile, is a prestigious section of downtown Chicago known for its luxury shops and architectural landmarks. It has one of the most beautiful skylines and has been noted for its exclusive lakefront hotels, museums, art, and culture.

There are many positive aspects of the city. Yet sadly, in recent years there has been a dramatic increase in violence and murders in Chicago. Last year alone there were over five hundred homicides.[1] The city has earned a reputation as one of the most violent in our nation as rival gangs kill to retaliate against one another and to instill fear.

As a graduate of an inner-city high school, I find it painful to turn on the news and hear of another beautiful, innocent child who has been gunned down by a stray bullet intended for someone else. I was recently invited to return to the high school that I graduated from to hear the president of the United States address the problem of urban violence. The mayor, governor, state officials, community leaders, chief of police, and clergy were also in attendance.

I sat quietly listening to the president try to offer some kind of solution. It seems that everyone is baffled by the increased level of anger, hostility, and violence among some of Chicago's youth. Young people in attendance that day said they felt the problem stemmed from the economic downturn and the difficulty many people have finding employment in the inner city. People had lots of theories about what would change the situation, but answers were few.

That day I met the mother of a young girl who had attended the president's inaugural festivities only to be murdered by random violence upon her return to Chicago. This young lady—an honor student with a bright future ahead of her—died while simply trying to shield herself from the rain. It broke my heart to think of the pain that girl's mother, family, and friends must feel. I am very empathetic for every parent who has been affected by the violence in our city.

Our ministry has periodically sent teams to minister in a juvenile correctional center. The young people were incarcerated for a variety of crimes. Some were arrested for selling or possessing drugs. Others committed murder or rape. We always observed a hardness and anger among the hundreds of youth we ministered to, but we continued to sing and preach the Word as if we were unfazed.

I remember once praying with a group of young people,

some of whom were gang members. I asked them why they were so angry and what caused them to lash out and hurt others. I cannot tell you how many times I heard the same reply: "They disrespected me." I heard this over and over again from both males and females. Remarkably, many of the girls were harder and angrier than the boys, and their arrests were for crimes just as violent as those committed by the young men.

The other common thread was that the youth were angry because their fathers were absent. I knew this was a significant contributor to juvenile crime, but the level of resentment expressed toward absentee fathers was astounding. Many times their single moms were forced to work long hours to provide food and shelter for their children. As a result, their children were being raised by teachers at school and babysitters, and they became targets for recruitment by gangs. In a number of cases neither parent was in the child's life because of drug abuse or incarceration, so the youth were being raised by elderly grandparents.

I have to say I was most surprised by the number of youth who complained of being disrespected. It amazed me that teenagers who had no jobs, major accomplishments, or meaningful reasons to command respect wanted that more than anything else. Respect is not demanded; it is earned. Youth today are complaining that there are no jobs, yet many dropped out of high school and aren't qualified for the positions that are available.

One of my sisters saw incredible success during her visits to the correctional center. My sister Denise is close to six feet tall, and the young people would call her "Big Neicy." Each time we visited, Big Neicy would bring the Word, and she commanded their attention. Denise has a remarkable ability to captivate young people. Her love and truthfulness have a way of disarming the most defensive person. Staff later told us that there was no violence or fighting for weeks after our visit. The facility's administrators called us back again and again because of the changes they were seeing in the youth.

Denise once asked a young Hispanic man if she could pray with him. He let her pray for him, and after she prayed, she asked if she could hug him. He gave her permission, and when she hugged him, he began to cry in her arms. He told her that he could not remember the last time his mother hugged him or told him that she loved him.

We see the violence in our streets, and we are right to be concerned. But if we want to see transformation in our cities, we must direct our prayers toward the spirit of violence working through broken, hurting individuals. We can pray for our youth caught up in these gangs to be free from the demonic powers that are terrorizing not only them but also their communities. We can pray for men to take their place as the prophets and priests of the home. And we can pray for our spiritual leaders who are ministering in our communities. We are not powerless in prayer. We can go boldly before the Lord, cast down strongholds, and set the captives free.

Prayer for Victims of Violence

Lord, in the midst of increasing violence and pain in our cities, we thank You that You are still God. We pray today for every family—every mother and father, every sibling and student—who has been affected by violence in our cities. Lord, we speak to the pain and hurt caused by the tragic homicides. We speak to the events that led to such a traumatic outcome.

Lord, only You know the depth of the heartache and pain felt by individuals who have lost family members and close friends in acts of senseless violence. Father, we ask that You extend Your hand of compassion and mercy to let healing begin. Lord, in Jesus's name we ask that You touch the hearts of the victims' families, that they will be able to release the anger and find peace.

We pray also for justice in every case. Lord, we ask that You work in the judicial system to bring every person responsible to a place of accountability and repentance. We pray for wisdom for every judge and attorney and that they will be instruments of justice. We ask, Lord, for the spirit of forgiveness to rest upon each person who has been devastated by acts of violence. We know if we regard bitterness in our hearts, You won't hear us when we pray.

We thank You, Lord, for breaking the spirit of violence and retaliation. Lord, we lift our youth in Your presence and pray that You will order their steps and keep them from the plan of the enemy.

Lord, we thank You for covering our family members and protecting them from this stronghold that is operating in our cities. We release the angels of the Lord to shield and protect Your children. We believe You will bring the victory in Jesus's name.

Lord, to every person who has been devastated and has an open wound, we apply the healing balm of Gilead to the place of pain. We ask, Lord, that You graciously give them peace and closure in the name of the Lord. Use the memory of the loved one to get the attention of our troubled youth.

God, grant them the serenity to accept the things we cannot change; courage to change the things we can; and wisdom to know the difference. Amen.[2]

Prayer for Men, the Prophets and Priests of the Family

Father, we intercede for men, the spiritual prophets and priests of the family. We intercede for men everywhere who have been under the attack of the enemy. We ask You now, Lord, to crown their heads with great wisdom and knowledge—wisdom for businesses and family decisions, and to know what direction You would have them to take. Your Word declares that the steps of a good man are ordered by You, so, Lord, we pray that You will make their pathway clear. Let the path be illuminated so that they may bring great glory unto You in the name of the Lord.

We pray for distinct spiritual clarity to hear Your voice. Anoint them to lead the family by example. We pray that they will respond to the promptings of the Holy Spirit. We ask that they would have a spirit of humility and sensitivity in every area. God, we ask that like Daniel they would have an excellent spirit and a strong dedication to prayer. Make them bold and fearless, Lord; give them courage like Gideon. And we pray that like Samuel they will respond to Your divine prompting.

We break every stronghold designed to influence men. Lord, help them to avoid the wrong path. Father, we rebuke every dominating Jezebel assignment and spirit. We bind every Ahab spirit of weakness designed to diminish their authority in the name of the Lord.

Lord, we come against the inability to make decisions and stand by them. We break every seducing spirit, like the assignment of Delilah that is sent to deceive and captivate. We curse the attempts of the enemy to discover the strengths You have given men and manipulate them. We bind every alluring and charming spirit that leads men away from Your principles and statutes and away from their families. We close every opening to low self-worth and low self-esteem that gives place to flattery and deceit.

Lord, let fathers be proper role models to their sons, and let the sons grow in the fear and admonition of the Lord. We say a special prayer for men whose fathers were absent during their adolescent years. We pray that You will be their heavenly Father who heals every disappointment. Fill every void left by the absence of a natural father, and give men the capacity to love You and their families the way they are supposed to. Holy Spirit, give them a forgiving spirit.

For every man of God, we pray the blessings of Abraham, Isaac, and Jacob upon them, and we ask for new streams of income and financial blessings. We release promotions and increase on their jobs. Father, bless them with money from unexpected sources for Your glory. We pray now that they will experience the unspeakable joy of the Lord. Bless every member of their families, and cover them in the precious shed blood of Jesus. Let this be a year of joy for their families. Bless them with time with their families to strengthen the bonds.

We pray for angelic protection and that the fathers will have a watchful eye to see the enemy afar off concerning the children. We thank You, Lord, for bountiful blessings and the release of agape love in Jesus's name. Amen.

Prayer for Spiritual Leaders

Lord, we cover every bishop, pastor, teacher, prophet, and evangelist who is spreading the good news of the gospel of Jesus Christ. Father, we speak grace and peace upon every man and woman of God who is serving faithfully in the church. Bless them now in the name of Jesus. We ask, Lord, that You touch their families to let them know they appreciate them for their work. Lord, let them know that they have Your approval and that You have made them victorious and more than conquerors.

Lord, touch the pastors today in a special way; so many have given their all for the sake of the ministry. God, You see and You care. Father, lift up the bowed-down head and give hope to that pastor who is in need. Provide natural and spiritual resources and give increase. We pray for property and land that their vision may come to pass. Father, we ask that You would raise up people of power and influence to help them achieve everything You have put in their hearts to do.

Give them everything You desire them to have. Bless their going out and their coming in. Give them increase this day in the mighty name that is above every name, to the glory of the Father. In Jesus's name, amen.

CONCLUSION

As I conclude the pages of *Spiritual Intervention*, it is my sincere hope that every word written will bless your life in a tremendous way. I believe these words were inspired by the Holy Spirit, and I believe that true intervention will occur for you and your loved ones. May the love of our abundant God surround you and fill you with exceeding joy. *"The Lord bless thee and keep thee: The Lord make his face shine upon thee, and be gracious unto thee: The Lord lift up his countenance upon thee, and give thee peace"* (Num. 6:24–26).

It would mean so much to me to hear how this book has been a blessing to you. I would love to receive your praise reports or testimonies of victory. You can write to Kimberly Ray at P. O. Box 1104, Matteson, IL 60443, or e-mail me at kray@angierayministries.com.

Appendix

STEPS TO ENTER INTO A PLACE OF PRAYER

After this manner therefore pray ye: Our Father which art
in heaven, hallowed be thy name. Thy kingdom come, thy
will be done in earth, as it is in heaven. Give us this day
our daily bread. And forgive us our debts, as we forgive our
debtors. And lead us not into temptation, but deliver us
from evil: For thine is the kingdom, and the power, and the
glory, for ever. Amen.

—Matthew 6:9–13

I N THE Lord's Prayer quoted above we find the steps we
should all keep in mind when we come before God's presence in prayer.

1. **Humbly honor God and pray with rever-
   ence and adoration.** *Our Father which art
   in heaven, hallowed be thy name (Matt. 6:9).*
   Psalm 100:4 tells us to enter into His gates
   with thanksgiving and into His courts with
   praise. **Ask in faith and with a submis-
   sive spirit for God's will to be done.** *Thy
   kingdom come, thy will be done in earth, as it is
   in heaven (Matt. 6:10).*

2. **Express your dependence upon the Lord
   and ask for His provision.** *Give us this day
   our daily bread (Matt. 6:11).*

3. **Ask the Lord for forgiveness of any sins
   of omission or commission.** *And forgive us
   our debts, as we forgive our debtors (Matt. 6:12).*
   Verses 14–15 go on to say, "For if ye forgive

men their trespasses, your heavenly Father will also forgive you: But if ye forgive not men their trespasses, neither will your Father forgive your trespasses."

4. **Ask the Lord to guide you and to keep you from the snares of the enemy.** *And lead us not into temptation, but deliver us from evil (Matt. 6:13).*

5. **Conclude by praising Him for who He is and the amazing things He has done.** *For thine is the kingdom, and the power, and the glory, for ever. Amen (Matt. 6:13).*

NOTES

Chapter 1—Not by Might nor Power

1. Merriam-Webster.com, s.v. "resist," http://www.merriam-webster.com/dictionary/resist (accessed September 15, 2013).

Chapter 2—Armed and Dangerous

1. Ibid., s.v. "war," http://www.merriam-webster.com/dictionary/war?show=0&t=1379306183 (accessed September 15, 2013).

2. Ibid., s.v. "principality," http://www.merriam-webster.com/dictionary/principality (accessed September 15, 2013).

3. Ibid., s.v. "power," http://www.merriam-webster.com/dictionary/power (accessed September 15, 2013).

Chapter 5—Eating Disorders

1. "Adult Obesity Facts," Centers for Disease Control and Prevention, August 13, 2012, http://www.cdc.gov/obesity/data/adult.html (accessed July 30, 2013).

Chapter 18—Violence in Our Cities

1. "Preliminary Annual Uniform Crime Report, January–December, 2012," Federal Bureau of Investigation, http://www.fbi.gov/about-us/cjis/ucr/crime-in-the-u.s/2012/preliminary-annual-uniform-crime-report-january-december-2012/tables/table-4-cuts/table_4_offenses_reported_to_law_enforcement_by_state_illinois_through_missouri_2012.xls (accessed September 15, 2013).

2. The Serenity Prayer is commonly attributed to Reinhold Neihbur, in his sermon delivered in 1943. For more information, see http://www.the-serenity-prayer.com/about_serenity.php (accessed September 15, 2013).

Kimberly Ray

Resources by Kimberly Ray

Prevailing Prayers of the Bible. This book was inspired by an amazing trip to Israel. I remember having the privilege to stand at the ancient Wailing Wall to pray. Honestly, I sensed an indescribable awe as I witnessed people praying. I observed a fascinating tradition—people placing slips of paper with prayer requests into the crevices of the Wailing Wall. This was an astonishing indication of their passion expressed to God through prayer and their belief that the prayers would be answered.

Relentless Faith. What is relentless faith? It is the kind of faith that resists the desire to concede to current circumstances. The Word of God is the answer to life's dilemma. Relentless Faith is faith in the Lord that is UNSHAKABLE, UNSTOPPABLE, and UNMOVABLE. This faith is never dependent upon our own abilities. It is a tenacious determination to embrace and believe the promises written in the Word of God. This relentless faith is connected to your core belief system.

Kimberly Ray

A Time of Intercession is a weekly telecast viewed on The Word Network, Monday nights @ 11:00 p.m. CST. Also viewed on The Total Living Network on Wednesday, Thursday, and Friday mornings. Check your local listing for time.

Other materials to strengthen to your prayer life include:

The Power of Agreement (DVD)
The Prayer Revival (DVD)
Prayer for the Family (DVD)
I Am Conditioned to Win (DVD)
Moments of Prayer (CD)

You are personally invited to visit
http://www.pastorkimberlyray.com/
www.angierayministries.com.

EMPOWERED
TO RADICALLY CHANGE
YOUR WORLD

Charisma House brings you books, e-books, and other media from dynamic Spirit-filled Christians who are passionate about God.

Check out all of our releases from best-selling authors like **Jentezen Franklin**, **Perry Stone**, **John Eckhardt**, and **Kimberly Daniels** and experience God's supernatural power at work.

CHARISMA
HOUSE

FREE NEWSLETTERS
TO HELP EMPOWER YOUR LIFE

Why subscribe today?

❑ **DELIVERED DIRECTLY TO YOU.** All you have to do is open your inbox and read.

❑ **EXCLUSIVE CONTENT.** We cover the news overlooked by the mainstream press.

❑ **STAY CURRENT.** Find the latest court rulings, revivals, and cultural trends.

❑ **UPDATE OTHERS.** Easy to forward to friends and family with the click of your mouse.

CHOOSE THE E-NEWSLETTER THAT INTERESTS YOU MOST:

- Christian news
- Daily devotionals
- Spiritual empowerment
- And much, much more

SIGN UP AT: **http://freenewsletters.charismamag.com**

8178